GET TRUMP

Also by Alan Dershowitz

Dershowitz on Killing

The Price of Principle

The Case for Vaccine Mandates

The Case for Color-Blind Equality in an Age of Identity Politics

The Case Against the New Censorship: Protecting Free Speech from Big Tech, Progressives, and Universities

Cancel Culture: The Latest Attack on Free Speech and Due Process

The Case for Liberalism in an Age of Extremism: or, Why I Left the Left But Can't Join the Right

Confirming Justice—Or Injustice?: A Guide to Judging RGB's Successor

Defending the Constitution

Guilt by Accusation: The Challenge of Proving Innocence in the Age of #MeToo

Defending Israel: The Story of My Relationship with My Most Challenging Client

The Case Against Impeaching Trump

The Case Against BDS: Why Singling Out Israel for Boycott Is Anti-Semitic and Anti-Peace

Trumped Up: How Criminalization of Political Differences Endangers Democracy

Electile Dysfunction: A Guide for Unaroused Voters

The Case Against the Iran Deal

Terror Tunnels: The Case for Israel's Just War Against Hamas

Abraham: The World's First (But Certainly Not Last) Jewish Lawyer

Taking the Stand: My Life in the Law

The Trials of Zion

The Case for Moral Clarity: Israel, Hamas and Gaza

The Case Against Israel's Enemies: Exposing Jimmy Carter and Others Who Stand in the Way of Peace

Is There a Right to Remain Silent? Coercive Interrogation and the Fifth Amendment After 9/11

Finding Jefferson: A Lost Letter, a Remarkable Discovery, and the First Amendment in the Age of Terrorism

Blasphemy: How the Religious Right is Hijacking Our Declaration of Independence

Pre-emption: A Knife That Cuts Both Ways

Rights From Wrongs: A Secular Theory of the Origins of Rights

America on Trial: Inside the Legal Battles That Transformed Our Nation

The Case for Peace: How the Arab-Israeli Conflict Can Be Resolved

The Case for Israel

America Declares Independence

Why Terrorism Works: Understanding the Threat, Responding to the Challenge

Shouting Fire: Civil Liberties in a Turbulent Age

Letters to a Young Lawyer

Supreme Injustice: How the High Court Hijacked Election 2000

Genesis of Justice: Ten Stories of Biblical Injustice that Led to the Ten Commandments and Modern Law

Just Revenge

Sexual McCarthyism: Clinton, Starr, and the Emerging Constitutional Crisis

The Vanishing American Jew: In Search of Jewish Identity for the Next Century

Reasonable Doubts: The Criminal Justice System and the O.J. Simpson Case

The Abuse Excuse: And Other Cop-Outs, Stories and Evasions of Responsibility

The Advocate's Devil

Contrary to Popular Opinion

Chutzpah

Taking Liberties: A Decade of Hard Cases, Bad Laws, and Bum Raps

Reversal of Fortune: Inside the Von Bülow Case

The Best Defense

Fair and Certain Punishment: Report of the 20th Century Fund Task Force on Criminal Sentencing

Courts of Terror: Soviet Criminal Justice and Jewish Emigration (coauthored with Telford Taylor)

Criminal Law: Theory and Process (with Joseph Goldstein and Richard Schwartz)

Psychoanalysis, Psychiatry, and Law (with Joseph Goldstein and Jay Katz)

GET TRUMP

THE THREAT TO CIVIL LIBERTIES, DUE PROCESS, AND OUR CONSTITUTIONAL RULE OF LAW

ALAN DERSHOWITZ

HOT BOOKS

Hot Books may be purchased in bulk at special discounts for sales promotion, corporate gifts, fund-raising, or educational purposes. Special editions can also be created to specifications. For details, contact the Special Sales Department, Skyhorse Publishing, 307 West 36th Street, 11th Floor, New York, NY 10018 or info@skyhorsepublishing.com

Hot Books® and Skyhorse Publishing® are registered trademarks of Skyhorse Publishing, Inc.®, a Delaware corporation.

Visit our website at www.skyhorsepublishing.com.

10 9 8 7 6 5 4 3

Library of Congress Cataloging-in-Publication Data is available on file.

Hardcover ISBN: 978-1-5107-7781-1
eBook: 978-1-5107-7782-8

Cover design by Brian Peterson

Printed in the United States of America

Dedication

This book is warmly dedicated to my student, mentee, mentor, colleague, and friend Harvey Silverglate—a great lawyer, an honest civil libertarian, and a paradigmatic mensch. One of the very few people who understands—and is willing to publicly defend my principled support for the Constitution, even on behalf of Donald Trump.

Acknowledgments

Thanks to Maura Kelly, Hector Carosso, and Tony Lyons for their help and support in producing this manuscript; to my dear wife Carolyn for inspiring, challenging, and constructively correcting me; and to Alan Rothfeld for keeping me on the grammatically and factually straight and narrow.

Contents

Introduction

Now that Donald Trump has announced his candidacy for reelection as president, the unremitting efforts by his political opponents to "get" him—to stop him from running—at any cost will only increase. These efforts may pose the most significant threat to civil liberties since McCarthyism. Though the end may seem commendable to many—stopping Trump from retaking the presidency—some of the means being advocated and employed challenge the very constitutional foundations of our liberty: due process, right to counsel, free speech, and the rule of law.

It is precisely because so many decent people honestly believe that a second Trump presidency would endanger our nation, that it is difficult to persuade them that their attacks on our cherished constitutional rights will cause enduring—perhaps irremediable—harm to our liberties. The fact that they may be right, at least to some degree, makes it more difficult to persuade many citizens that the danger to our constitutional rights may be deeper and more enduring. They see the threat posed by Trump as concrete and immediate, whereas the threat to our liberties is more abstract and long term. But history teaches us that ends, even if believed to be noble, do not justify ignoble means that are inconsistent with democracy and the rule of law.

Lifelong civil libertarians and liberals, who have been suspicious of prosecutors, the FBI, and congressional investigatory committees, have suddenly become their most ardent supporters, advocating even more aggressive and repressive tactics—so long as they are directed at "getting" Trump. Defenders of Trump's constitutional rights—even those like me who oppose him politically—are sought to be silenced; their free speech rights attacked, their integrity questioned, and their careers threatened.

Much of the media substitutes advocacy against Trump for objective reporting, while many in academia petition and propagandize against rights they previously valued—all in the interest of getting Trump. Those who praised John Adams for defending the British soldiers accused of the Boston massacre, former Justice Benjamin Curtis for defending Andrew Johnson, and James St. Clair for defending Richard Nixon, now turn on those of us who have defended the Constitution on behalf of Donald Trump. Trump is "different" and those who defend his rights, like those who defended the rights of accused communists during McCarthyism, must be counted as enablers or coconspirators who themselves should be held responsible for the evils attributed to their clients.

They deny that they are hypocrites, applying an immoral double standard. Because Trump is "different"—and the dangers he poses more serious—a different standard is justified. They are righteous in their willingness, indeed eagerness, to bend or even break the constitution in order to prevent a greater evil. That claim has been made throughout history by zealots determined to thwart what they regard as dangerous.

Those out to get Trump are willing to weaponize and distort our criminal justice system to target their political enemy. Perhaps the most extreme instance of this dangerous phenomenon was the effort of Professor Laurence Tribe, my former colleague at Harvard Law School, to persuade Attorney General Merrick Garland to prosecute Trump for attempting to murder former vice president Mike Pence, despite the absence of any plausible legal basis for such a prosecution.

On account of today's fears, these "Get Trumpers" ignore the implications for tomorrow of their anti-libertarian actions. They believe that because Trump is a scoundrel—or worse—he must be stopped at all costs. The Constitution and civil liberties be damned because they are merely technical barriers to the more important goal of ridding our nation of the influence of Trump.

They have forgotten the lesson of history well summarized by H. L. Mencken: "The trouble with fighting for human freedom is that one spends most of one's time defending scoundrels. For it is against scoundrels that oppressive laws are first aimed, and oppression must be stopped at the beginning if it is to be stopped at all."

The "Get Trump" posse not only advocates the deployment of oppressive laws against Trump and his "enablers," they actually want to expand the reach of such dangerous laws so that they can encompass President Trump. A prime example of this attitude is The Espionage Act of 1917, which has long been the object of criticism, derision, and hatred by civil libertarians and liberals, because its vague and open-ended language was used for decades against left-wing icons such as Eugene V. Debs, Emma Goldman, Benjamin Spock, Daniel Ellsberg, Julian Assange, and others. Now many of these same leftists demand that its scope be expanded even further to reach Trump. If the shoe doesn't fit on the other foot, stretch it to fit your political enemies, especially Trump.

The essence of justice is that it must be equally applicable to all. Targeting individuals, even scoundrels, violates the core principles of justice that go back to the Bible, which warns against "recogniz[ing] faces" (*lo takir panim*)—hence the statue of justice blindfolded and holding balanced scales. Our Constitution promises the equal protection of the law and prohibits bills of attainder, which were employed by the British parliament to mete out punishment to named individuals who were deemed dangerous to the state. A South American dictator once said that "for my friends everything, for my enemies the law." Weaponizing the law to target political enemies is the way of tyrannies not democracies. As Lavrentiy Beria, the notorious head of the Soviet KGB assured Stalin: "Show me the man and I will find you the crime."

Today "the man" is Donald Trump. And the "Get Trump" radicals are desperately trying to "find" crimes—or in some instances, like Tribe's attempted-murder fantasy, to simply make them up. They may succeed if they persist in their desperate quest, because as my friend and colleague Harvey Silverglate has observed in his masterful book *Three Felonies a Day*: "Every Soviet citizen committed at least three felonies a day, because the criminal statutes were written so broadly as to cover ordinary day-to-day activities. The Communist Party decided whom to prosecute from among the millions of possible criminals." American law is not so open-ended or discretionary, but statutory crimes such as conspiracy, obstruction, RICO, espionage, sedition, mishandling of secrets, and election laws are vague enough to allow partisan abuse of discretion. As Justice Robert Jackson, a former prosecutor, cautioned about American criminal law, "With the law books filled with a great assortment of crimes, a prosecutor stands a fair chance of finding at least a technical violation of some act on the part of almost anyone. In such a case, it is not a question of discovering the commission of a crime and then looking for the man who has committed it, it is a question of picking the man and then searching the law books, or putting investigators to work, to pin some offense on him." This is an especially dangerous approach when a special prosecutor is appointed to investigate and possibly prosecute a named individual.

Searching for crimes or manufacturing them is antithetical to democracy, but especially so if the target is likely to run against the incumbent president in the coming election. No one is above the law but digging to find crimes in order to influence an election does not constitute the equal application of the law. In order to assure equal application in comparable situations, I have proposed two criteria for indicting a likely candidate of the opposing party: the Richard Nixon standard and the Hillary Clinton standard.

The first requires a bipartisan consensus: Nixon's crimes were so serious and obvious that leaders of his own party demanded his resignation—or impeachment and prosecution. He destroyed evidence, bribed, paid hush money, and engaged in other activities that clearly constituted core obstructions of justice and other crimes. In today's deeply divisive climate, it is unlikely that this standard could literally be met: many Republican leaders are unlikely to agree that Trump should be prosecuted, regardless of the evidence of criminality. But a reasonable variation on that standard would be that the evidence of serious criminality is so clear that a considerable number of Republicans would agree that he should be prosecuted, thus eliminating the plausibility of the claim that his prosecution was merely a partisan attempt to affect the next presidential election. The January 6 Committee of the House of Representatives included two carefully selected Republicans who want Trump prosecuted, but neither of them can be deemed mainstream members of Trump's own party: one was defeated in the Republican primary; the other resigned his seat.

For the second standard to be met, the evidence of Trump's criminality would have to be well beyond the level of Hillary Clinton's mishandling of classified and other national security material. Clinton was the Democratic candidate for president while her investigation was ongoing. She was not prosecuted, despite allegations that she possessed and destroyed sensitive material. Some of these allegations are disputed, but so are some of the allegations against Trump. Although Clinton wasn't prosecuted, improper statements made by former FBI director James Comey may well have influenced her electoral defeat. But it is the absence of any prosecution rather than the presence of inappropriate FBI statements, that is the critical factor. If the American public reasonably believes that Trump's legal misbehavior is roughly equivalent to Clinton's, many will see this as the application of a double standard based on partisan considerations.

This standard applies specifically to Trump's post-presidential possession of classified documents, but it is applicable as well to other alleged misconduct that has not been prosecuted when committed by others.

Meeting these standards is especially important since Trump may be running for president against the incumbent who nominated top justice department officials. These officials must be scrupulous to avoid an actual injustice, but also the appearance of injustice. The appointment of a special prosecutor by Attorney General Merrick Garland was designed to eliminate this concern.

The "Get Trump" camp is making it difficult for Merrick Garland to do and to appear to be doing justice. These extremists not only don't care about the equal application of the law, but they also demand a double standard against Trump precisely because they believe that Trump is more dangerous and more evil than Hillary Clinton was. (Many anti-Clinton zealots believed the opposite.) The pressure on Garland to prosecute Trump, especially from the left of his party, may be irresistible. At the very least, it will subject any prosecutorial decision to the accusation that it was influenced by the "Get Trump" zealotry.

Nor was this danger eliminated by Garland's appointment of a special prosecutor to investigate President Biden's allegedly improper possession of classified material after he left the vice presidency. The appointment was designed to create the appearance of justice and equality. But a sitting president cannot be criminally prosecuted, while a former president can. It is unlikely that either will be indicted for the mishandling of classified information, but Trump is also being investigated for other alleged crimes related to his challenging the results of the election and the events of January 6.

In addition to targeting Donald Trump himself, the "Get Trump" campaign is also out to get his lawyers and anyone associated with him. The targeting of his lawyers is especially troubling, since it implicates the Sixth Amendment right to effective assistance of counsel. Good lawyers are understandably afraid of becoming the subjects of criminal or bar investigation if they dare to defend Trump. Even I, who has never been suspected or accused of any misconduct during my representation of Trump in the Senate, have been subject to punishment, cancellation, and a bar complaint. My family, too, has been attacked. Several first-rate lawyers have told me that they don't want to be "Dershowitzed"—that is, subjected to the kind of punishments to which I have been subjected.

Recently, the FBI has seized the telephones of some of Trump's lawyers (and others). As a result, there have been calls for these lawyers to recuse themselves because of a conflict of interest. This reminds me of what I experienced in the Soviet Union during the late 1960s and early 1970s when I represented dissidents and refuseniks. Whenever I retained a Soviet lawyer to assist me, that lawyer would be investigated and sometimes even deported. Deportation from the Soviet Union was not always a bad thing, and some Jewish lawyers volunteered to assist me precisely in order to be deported! But this is not the Soviet Union, and American lawyers do not want to be investigated or prosecuted.

We experienced a similar reaction during McCarthyism, when American lawyers were punished for representing accused communists and fellow travelers. Many good lawyers, law firms, and legal organizations refused to represent the victims of McCarthyism because they didn't want to be investigated or tainted with the accusation that they must be communists, fellow travelers, or sympathizers if they are willing to defend them. When I was in college, I was a fervent anti-communist, but I defended the rights of accused communists to teach and speak. This led the right-wing president of the college to refuse to recommend me for a Rhodes and other scholarships. Today, I am opposed to many of Trump's policies, but I defend his constitutional rights, so I too am accused by leftists of being a Trump supporter and enabler. Even one of my oldest childhood friends wrote me that, "It's pretty obvious that your pro-Trump bias is influencing your viewpoints, just wish I could figure out why?" It apparently never occurred to him that my viewpoints have always been influenced by civil liberties for all!

Lawyers must be encouraged to represent people with whom they disagree politically and ideologically, lest only sympathizers will represent controversial defendants. Today, lawyers are discouraged and worse from defending those with whom they disagree. This has been especially problematic when it comes to representing Trump and/or his associates. What is true of Trump today may be true in the future of controversial Democrats. Our legal system is based on precedent, and there are only two alternatives: precedent will be followed and will end up compromising the rights of future public figures; or precedent will not be followed and will turn the law into an ad hoc weapon that can selectively target political opponents. Justice Robert Jackson once criticized a Supreme Court decision for being ad hoc and not creating a precedent, analogizing it to a limited train ticket: for this day and time only. The High Court in *Bush v. Gore* opened itself to similar criticism when the majority went out of its way to say that "our consideration is limited" to the "present circumstances."

Neither alternative is acceptable in a democracy governed by the rule of law.

In at least one respect, the current attacks on our fundamental rights by "Get Trump" zealots are even more dangerous than the past attacks on our fundamental rights by McCarthyites. McCarthyites were generally old men who represented America's past. McCarthyism lasted less than a decade and its effects were quickly overcome (except on those who were permanently injured). Many victims of McCarthyism were glorified when it ended. The marvelous film *The Front* captures both the evils of McCarthyism and the aftermath. The film itself was written, directed, and acted by blacklisted artists.

The lessons learned from McCarthyism have stayed with us for a considerable amount of time. Tragically, however, they have not been learned—or at least accepted—by the "Get Trump" brigade. Moreover, those who are advocating and practicing the elimination or reduction of civil liberties in their efforts to get Trump tend to be younger and more representative of the future of America. They include many teachers who are propagandizing our future leaders into a distain for inconvenient constitutional rights that are seen as hindrances to their utopian progress. They fail, or refuse, to see the dystopian future that their attitudes and actions threaten to impose on our nation. This attitude is not limited to the current "Get Trump" movement. It applies more broadly to civil liberties in general, especially freedom of speech and due process for those who stand in the way of "woke progress."

For the first time in my adult life, people who have long claimed to be liberals, civil libertarians, and proponents of the rule of law are explicitly trashing the Constitution and diminishing the importance of our basic rights. If they represent our future, it is indeed bleak.

Many of those who are engaged in this "Get Trump" at any cost effort seek to justify it by saying "this is different." They truly believe that never before in our history, have we faced threats comparable to those we face from election of Donald Trump in 2024. As Jesse Wegman wrote in a *New York Times* op-ed arguing that Trump is ineligible to run because he "engaged in insurrection or rebellion": "I am open to using any constitutional means of preventing him from even attempting to return to the White House."[1] This apparently includes stretching the words and intent of the Constitution to fit this "different" situation. But history teaches us that every effort to deny basic rights and civil liberties has been justified by the claim that "this is different." The Alien and Sedition Acts were passed because the threat from France was "different." Lincoln suspended the writ of habeas corpus because the threat of a Confederate victory was "different." Wilson authorized the Parker Raids because the threat of anarchy was "different." Roosevelt confined 110,000 Japanese Americans because the threat from Japan was "different." McCarthyism was justified because the

---

1 Jesse Wegman, "Is Donald Trump Ineligible to Be President?," *New York Times*, November 24, 2022, https://www.nytimes.com/2022/11/24/opinion/trump-14th-amendment.html.

threat of communism was "different." The overreaction to the sometimes-violent protests against the Vietnam War was justified because that threat was "different." The attempt to suppress publication of the Pentagon Papers was explained to the Supreme Court because the release of these papers would be "different." The acceptance of practices such as waterboarding and lengthy detentions following the attacks of 9/11 was justified because terrorism is "different." Now we hear that the threat would be "different" in the event that Americans decide to reelect Trump.

We are told that the Constitution is not a suicide pact, but nor is it a document that can be ignored simply because things are "different." It is the longest serving written Constitution in recorded history. It has survived so long because it has adapted to changing circumstances. It has generally done so by expanding rights rather than contracting them. Professor Tribe exaggerated when he described the decision overruling *Roe v. Wade* as being the first time Americans went to sleep at night with fewer rights than they had when they woke up. But it is no exaggeration to say that rarely in our history have so many purported civil libertarians, including Tribe, been willing to compromise basic rights in order to prevent the election of a candidate who would pose dangers that are "different."

We have survived the election of very bad public officials including presidents. We have survived attacks from enemies both abroad and at home. It would be remarkable if the event that succeeded in diminishing our rights was the fear of electing a disfavored candidate such as Donald Trump.

I have voted against Trump twice and I demand my constitutional right to vote against him a third time if he is nominated. That fundamental right should not be taken away from me or from those who would vote for him by "Get Trump" citizens or bureaucrats who are prepared to weaponize our system of justice in order to prevent his election.

Democrats and Republicans, liberals and conservatives, old and young, black and white, should all remain united against efforts to undercut democracy by employing tactics that personify totalitarian regimes: namely, selectively searching for and finding technical, obscure, or questionable crimes and other tactics that could be charged against opposing candidates.

Some of my closest friends—who I love and admire—consistently write me urging that I stop defending Trump's rights. They honestly fear that Trump's election will turn us into a totalitarian regime. They fail to understand how effective our system of checks and balances has been and continues to be, as a bulwark against any one person becoming a tyrant. There is no guarantee that the election of Trump would not produce bad results. That is why I plan to vote against him. Nor is it guaranteed that our institutions of governance will fully protect us from a potential tyrant. Learned Hand reminded us that when the spirit of liberty dies among citizens, no institutions can save it. The hard question is which result is more likely to kill our spirit of liberty: the election of Trump; or the attack on our liberties in an effort to prevent his election. In the pages to come—which consist of op-eds and interviews in roughly chronological order and updated by reference to current events—I express my strong views that we can survive Trump, but that it is less certain that we can survive the current attacks on our basic rights being advocated and engineered by those who would try to get Trump at any cost.

CHAPTER 1

The Search of Trump's Home

—————

In August of 2022, the FBI conducted a wide-ranging search of Mar-a-Largo, seizing many documents. I wrote critically of the government's actions.

Justice Department Should Have Subpoenaed Documents, Not Raided Trump's Home

The decision by the Justice Department to conduct a full-scale morning raid on former president Trump's Mar-a-Lago home does not seem justified, based on what we know as of now. If it is true that the basis of the raid was the former president's alleged removal of classified material from the White House, that would constitute a double standard of justice.

There were no raids, for example, on the homes of Hillary Clinton or former Clinton administration national security adviser Sandy Berger for allegations of mishandling official records in the recent past. Previous violations of the

Presidential Records Act typically have been punished by administrative fines, not criminal prosecution. Perhaps there are legitimate reasons for applying a different standard to Trump's conduct, but those are not readily obvious at this stage.

The more appropriate action would have been for a grand jury to issue a subpoena for any boxes of material that were seized and for Trump's private safe that was opened. That would have given Trump's lawyers the opportunity to challenge the subpoena on various grounds—that some of the material was not classified; that previous classified material was declassified by Trump; that other documents may be covered by various privileges, such as executive or lawyer-client.

Instead, the FBI apparently seized everything in view and will sort the documents and other material without a court deciding which ones are appropriately subject to Justice Department seizure.

Searches and seizures should only be used when subpoenas are inappropriate because of the risk of evidence destruction. It is important to note that Trump himself was a thousand miles away when the FBI's search and seizure occurred. It would have been impossible, therefore, for him to destroy subpoenaed evidence, especially if the subpoena demanded immediate production. If he or anyone else destroyed evidence that was subject to a subpoena, that would be a far more serious crime than what the search warrant seems to have alleged. It is unlikely that there is a basis for believing that the search warrant was sought because of a legitimate fear that subpoenaed evidence would be destroyed.

Defenders of the raid argue that the search warrant was issued by a judge. Yet every criminal defense lawyer knows that search warrants are issued routinely and less critically than candy is distributed on Halloween; judges rarely exercise real discretion or real supervision. It may be different when a president's home is the object of the search, but only time will tell whether that was the case here.

Neutral, objective justice must not only be done, but it must also be *seen* to be done.

For zealous Trump haters, anything done to Trump is justified. For zealous Trump lovers, nothing done to him is ever justified. For the majority of moderate, thoughtful Americans, however, the Justice Department's raid likely seems—at least at this point in time—to be unjust or needlessly confrontational.

Thus, it is now up to the Justice Department and the FBI to justify their actions to the American public. They must explain why a different standard appears to have been applied to Democrats such as Clinton and Berger than to Republicans such as Trump and many of his associates.

Critics of this demand for a single standard of justice insultingly call it "whataboutism." A more appropriate term would be "the shoe on the other foot test." No government act should ever be accepted unless it would be equally applied if the shoe were on the other foot—in other words, if it were applied equally to political friends and foes. This is the essence of our constitutional requirement of the equal protection of the law.

For now, let's not rush to judgment. Let's give the attorney general, Merrick Garland, and the director of the FBI, Christopher Wray, the opportunity to explain their actions. If they decline to do so, on the basis of confidentiality, a special master should be appointed by the relevant court to assess the evidence seized from Trump's home on a confidential basis. In the alternative, a true congressional committee comprised of both Democrats and Republicans should be appointed to investigate this raid.

It is true that a president or former president is not above the law—but neither should he or she be *below* the law. Precedents established in relation to Democrats must be equally applied to Republicans. On the face of it, this standard has not been met here.

The burden of proof is now on the Justice Department and the FBI to justify what appears to be unequal justice.

Appointing a Special Master

Judge Aileen Cannon was correct to reject the Justice Department's "trust us" argument that its "taint team" was sufficient to protect former president Trump's rights. The rights at stake are important: lawyer-client and executive privileges, both of which are rooted in the Constitution. The taint team is comprised of Justice Department officials who report to the same attorney general to whom the trial prosecutors report. The self-serving justification for a taint team is that Justice Department lawyers should be trusted to keep from other Justice Department lawyers the content of privileged material.

Assume for argument's sake that the taint team discovered a smoking gun document—say an admission by Trump to his personal lawyer that he had deliberately destroyed several subpoenaed documents. This unlikely admission would be privileged, since it involves a communication about past, not future crime.

Could every member of the Justice Department taint team be trusted not to communicate it by a wink or nod to the Justice Department trial lawyers?

Or consider a more salacious hypothetical admission, say a past affair with a Russian agent. This too would be privileged. Could the taint team be trusted to not leak such a juicy tidbit to a friendly journalist who would be protected against revealing the source?

Many Americans would want to see such information disclosed. But the law, for better or worse, requires that it be kept secret. If the law were changed to permit disclosure, clients would not make such admissions to their lawyers. In that case, lawyers would be unable not only to defend their clients effectively; they would also be unable to try to persuade their clients to do the right thing—such as disclosing their derelictions in order to minimize the damage.

The same would be true of executive privileged information. The Biden administration, backed by its reliable academic justifiers, argue that an incumbent president is empowered to waive the executive privilege of a former president who is his likely opponent in the upcoming election. What president would ever confide in a staff member knowing that his successor and future opponent can waive his privilege to achieve a partisan electoral advantage? Yet this is what these biased "experts" are advocating—so long as the holder of the executive privilege is Trump. You can be sure that many of them would be arguing the exact opposite if the holder of the privilege were Biden and his successor were Trump, who was waving Biden's privilege.

This is what it's come to in American media, academia, and politics. Arguments aren't made or judged on their merits or demerits. The only criteria are which side is benefited by how the issue is decided. A winning argument on its merits will be attacked if it is made by the wrong person or party. A losing argument will be praised if it helps the right person or party.

The Bible commands us not to "recognize faces" when trying to do justice. Hence the blindfolded statue holding the scales of justice. But there are no blindfolds or scales today. Justice is what helps your friends and hurts your enemies. The thumb of partisanship weighs too heavily on the scales of Justice. Neutral principles used to be praised. Now they are condemned as implicitly favoring the status quo, the powerful and the entitled. The Constitution has been trashed in the false name of "equity" and reparations. The rule of law has been weaponized against meritocracy and color-blind equality.

Getting back to Judge Cannon's decision to appoint a special master, there is scant debate on the merits or demerits of her decision. The discussion focuses on whether it makes it more difficult to "get" Trump. Civil libertarians who have traditionally distrusted the justice department to monitor itself are suddenly defending internal "taint teams." Instead of being skeptical of FBI intrusions on due process, they are calling for more intrusive measures against former president Trump. They are not even embarrassed that their partisan hypocrisy is so obvious. The shoe doesn't have to fit on Trump's foot, as long as it can be used to kick him to the ground. This is not blindfolded justice.

[The United States Court of Appeals for the 11th Circuit reversed Judge Cannon's decision—erroneously in my view.]

The Trump Affidavit: Four Conclusions on Guilt and Evidence

Reading the unredacted portions of the affidavit and appendices which the FBI used to search Donald Trump's Mar-a-Lago residence, leads to some initial conclusions.

The affidavit contains sufficient factual basis for Magistrate Judge Reinhardt to find probable cause to issue a search warrant. The standard for issuing a search warrant is very low, and any federal or magistrate judge would have issued a warrant based on the unredacted information contained in the affidavit. So, Magistrate Judge Reinhardt should not be criticized for his decision to issue the warrant.

The affidavit and the appendices seem exceptionally broad and virtually unlimited. It excludes rooms at the Mar-a-Lago complex used by third parties—guests and members of the club—but extends to virtually every other area where boxes could be stored. The search warrant itself also seems, to me, to be overly broad and inconsistent with the Fourth Amendment's requirement of "particularly describing the place to be searched and the person or things to be seized."

The actual search itself may even have exceeded the terms of the warrant, if it is true that it extended to Mrs. Trump's personal closet and other private areas, absent evidence that relevant material was stored there.

Most importantly, the unredacted portions of the affidavit do not seem to justify the decision of the Justice Department—as distinguished from the decision of the judge—to seek a warrant, instead of pursuing the subpoena route. There was probable cause for obtaining a search warrant early in the year, yet none was sought. And even when the search warrant was obtained, it was not executed for two days, thus suggesting the absence of real urgency.

It is precisely because search warrants are so easy to obtain that Attorney General Merrick Garland correctly stated that the Justice Department should seek them only when there is no other reasonable option. The unredacted portions of the affidavit do not seem to meet Garland's own standard.

Finally, the unredacted portions of the affidavit suggest there may be enough evidence to seek and obtain the indictment of former president Trump. Yet, once again, the standard for obtaining an indictment is very low. As a former judge of the New York Court of Appeals once said: "A prosecutor can get a grand jury to indict a ham sandwich."

It is precisely because it is so easy to obtain an indictment that prosecutorial discretion is so important. As a pure matter of technicality, there probably was enough evidence to secure an indictment of Hillary Clinton; a grand jury would certainly have accepted a prosecutor's decision to do so. But the decision was made not to seek an indictment in her case. That was the correct decision back then—and it would be the correct decision now, too, if the evidence is no greater than that present in the redacted affidavit. It is possible that the redacted portions would provide evidence that satisfies the Nixon and Clinton standards (see pages 5–7)—but the unredacted portions do not seem to do so.

All of these conclusions are based on a quick preliminary review of the unredacted portions of the affidavit; my views may change, depending on whether more information is forthcoming. But based on what I have read, and my fifty years of experience in reading similar documents, these are my conclusions.

Here's Why Trump Wasn't Just Subpoenaed

I now know why former president Donald Trump's papers were seized in a search, rather than obtained via subpoena. It was to circumvent his Fifth Amendment rights.

If Trump were subpoenaed to turn over material that may be classified, his lawyers would have the right to claim that the very act of producing these documents would be incriminating. It would constitute an admission that he possessed these contraband documents. This is a common problem in criminal investigations. The Justice Department generally solves the problem by offering the suspect "production immunity." This is a rather complex constitutional mechanism, but it is one that is frequently used. If a defendant is given production immunity, he must turn over the incriminating documents, but the government is precluded from using the fact that it was he who turned them over. The government remains free to introduce the documents for their substantive content—but the government cannot say whence it obtained them, and it cannot use the fact that the source produced them as evidence of the source's guilt.

The Justice Department obviously did not want to give Trump production immunity, so it deliberately circumvented his Fifth Amendment rights by simply seizing them when he was a thousand miles away. Since it was not Trump or his lawyers who turned them over, Trump cannot claim his

Fifth Amendment rights were violated. This is very clever, perhaps, but it is also highly questionable.

Obviously, any jury would easily infer where the documents were when they were seized. It really makes little practical difference whether Trump or his lawyers handed them over, or whether they were merely found on his premises. But the courts have decided that this distinction matters.

It didn't always matter. And in the famous trial of Aaron Burr for treason, Burr refused to comply with a subpoena, claiming that the content of the subpoenaed documents was incriminating. Supreme Court Chief Justice John Marshall accepted that argument and quashed the subpoena. But in subsequent cases since, the courts have legally distinguished between the incriminating *contents* of documents, on the one hand, and the active *production* itself, on the other hand.

How many angels can dance on the tip of a pin? But on the answer to such questions does the law often make fine distinctions.

If I am right, then the question raised is whether it is proper to use a search to deny a potential defendant his Fifth Amendment right against self-incrimination. Proponents of a search would argue that since he had no legitimate claim of self-incrimination in the *contents* of the papers themselves, he has lost no Fifth Amendment right by the search. Opponents of a search designed to circumvent the self-incrimination would respond by arguing that the purported content/production distinction is a distinction without a real difference.

Proponents of the search will probably win in court, if the magistrate judge reasonably found that there was probable cause. But they may well lose in the court of public opinion, where this esoteric legal distinction will not be understood or justified.

There may be another reason why a subpoena was not issued, and a search and seizure conducted instead. A subpoena must be for specific documents. A search, by contrast, can be more sweeping and may discover incriminating evidence that was not directly sought by the warrant but is deemed to be in "plain view." The search may also have been designed to send a message that the Justice Department is playing hardball, and that it will use every tactic at its disposal to intimidate Trump and his lawyers.

These issues will ultimately be resolved in a court of law. But if the goal of those employing these tactics is to prevent Trump from running for president again or to negatively affect his chances if he does run, these tactics may well backfire in the court of public opinion.

The administration of justice is not a game. The rules must not only be fair, but they must be perceived by the public as fair. They must also be seen to be applied equally. These tactics were not used against Hillary Clinton or Sandy Berger for comparable violations of the relevant underlying statutes. So even if these tactics can be justified in the abstract, they still may not reflect the equal protection—and equal enforcement—of the law.

Is This the End of Executive Privilege? Or Only for Trump?

In its appeal from Judge Aileen Cannon's order appointing a special master, the Biden administration is taking the position that the incumbent president can waive claims of executive privilege by his predecessor even if his predecessor is likely to run against him in the next election. So, let's see how this would have played out if the shoe were on the other foot.

Imagine if President Donald Trump had tried to waive his predecessor's executive privilege, relating to President Barack Obama's decision to allow the United Nations Security Council to condemn Israel for its continuing "occupation" of the Western Wall and the roads to Hebrew University and Hadassah Hospital. Many in the Obama administration opposed this one-sided resolution as anti-Israel and wanted the United States to veto it, as it had vetoed previous anti-Israel resolutions. But Obama instructed his UN representative, Samantha Powers, not to veto it.

Trump knew he would be running against Obama's vice president and that he might gain an electoral advantage if Congress held hearings on the controversial Obama decision. What advice did Biden give Obama? Is it true that Powers wanted to veto the resolution, but Obama forbade it in order to take revenge against Israeli Prime Minister Benjamin Netanyahu for his speech opposing the Iran deal?

Disclosing these privileged negotiations might well have hurt Biden with pro-Israel voters.

What if Obama had been called by a congressional committee to turn over all internal communications—written and oral—regarding his decision, and he claimed executive privilege? And what if then-president Trump was to have waived Obama's privilege?

One thing we know to be certain: many of the academic *experts* and media *pundits* who now support the argument that an incumbent president can waive the executive privilege of his predecessor would be making exactly the opposite argument. They would be saying—as I am saying now—that presidents would be reluctant to have confidential communications with their aides if they knew these communications could be made public by their successor in order to gain partisan electoral advantage. It would essentially mark the end of executive privilege, which is rooted in Article II of the Constitution.

The weaponization of the Constitution and the law for partisan advantage has become so pervasive, especially in academia and the media, that predicting what position many experts and pundits will take is no longer possible on the basis of neutral principles or precedents, since these have ceased to be the basis for their positions. Accurate predictions today require us to know which persons or parties will be helped or hurt by particular outcomes. Hypocrisy reigns. And those who engage in it are not even embarrassed when their double standards are exposed. The current *principle* is that the ends justify the means, especially if the end is the end of Trump.

Nor are Democrats the only guilty party. Perhaps the most blatant example of partisan hypocrisy was how the Republican Senate treated the 2016 nomination of Merrick Garland and the 2020 nomination of Amy Coney Barrett as Supreme Court justices. The Republicans refused to give Garland a hearing in 2016, because it was too close to the election, but then rushed through the nomination of Barrett just weeks before the 2020 election. Whenever asked to justify their obvious double standard, their only response was "because we can."

"Because we can" has become the current mantra of both parties. Neutral principles, which apply equally without regard to partisan advantage, are for wimps, not party leaders or other government officials. "They do it too" has become the excuse du jour. Both parties do it, but that is not a valid excuse even in hardball politics. Two constitutional violations do not cancel each other. They only make things worse.

Executive privilege is important to both parties—and to the constitutional rule of law. Today's partisan victory for Democrats, if their waiver argument is accepted, will soon become their loss should Republicans take control.

So, beware of what you wish for. Today's dream may well become tomorrow's nightmare.

CHAPTER 2

Investigating and Punishing Trump Supporters

S everal of Trump's lawyers and advisors have been investigated and or indicted. Bar complaints were filed against
me and others by a highly partisan group called the "65
Project" (see pages 44–46). I wrote several articles about
whether this was the product of a double standard of justice.

Giuliani's Suspension from the Law
Is Unconstitutional

Rudy Giuliani has been suspended from the practice of
law without a hearing, based largely on First Amendment–
protected statements he made outside of any court of law.
A panel of the Appellate Division of New York suspended
the former mayor of New York and former United States
attorney without giving him an opportunity to dispute the
charges against him at an evidentiary hearing. Moreover, he

was suspended largely on the basis of statements he made not in court but on television.

I am particularly familiar with many of his statements because I am advising the legal team representing MyPillow CEO Mike Lindell, who is being sued for defamation by Dominion Voting Systems, regarding Lindell's own comments about the 2020 election.

Although Giuliani is now entitled to a post-suspension hearing, it seems clear that the judges already have made up their minds, saying that the result will "likely" be "substantial permanent sanctions"—which means disbarment.

The courts have long held that a lawyer is not entitled to the full protection of the First Amendment for statements made in court. That may be understandable because a lawyer has a special obligation to be candid with judges and jurors.

But there are no compelling arguments why anyone—lawyer or non-lawyer—should be denied the full protection of the First Amendment when he or she participates in the marketplace of ideas on television, podcasts, or other media, even when representing a client.

Any statements made in such a public context can be rebutted in the marketplace of ideas, and so the public needs no special protection from statements made by lawyers. This is especially true when the statements concern important and controversial political events like an election.

There is no doubt that Giuliani's media statements, if made by a non-lawyer, would have been fully protected by the First Amendment, even if false. This is so for two reasons: every citizen should have the right to express controversial opinions—even wrong-headed ones—about a contested election; and every citizen should have the right to hear such views and make up their own minds.

Consider the controversy over the cause of the spread of COVID-19: Initially, people were sanctioned on social media platforms for suggesting that the virus may have originated in a research lab in China. Now, that still-unproven theory has been widely accepted—and widely discussed—as a real possibility, because the marketplace of ideas and information changed minds.

The rules under which Giuliani has been suspended are so vague that they cannot possibly satisfy the standards of due process, especially where public speech is concerned, and clarity is required before it is suppressed.

The court cited a rule allowing disbarment for conduct, including speech that "adversely reflects on the lawyer's fitness as a lawyer." It is difficult to imagine a more subjective standard that invites selective application. The panel also cited a rule that called for disbarment for knowingly making "false statements of fact or law to a third person."

If these rules were applied across the board fairly, and equitably, thousands of lawyers would be disbarred every year. I personally know of dozens of lawyers who seemingly have violated these rules. Lying and exaggeration are all too common in plea-bargaining, negotiations, and soliciting clients. And yet these sins are never the basis for discipline against recidivating lawyers. I can document dozens of similar cases where disciplinary boards in New York and elsewhere have done nothing to lawyers who have committed misconduct far more egregious than that alleged against Giuliani, including prosecutorial misconduct that resulted in the conviction of innocent defendants. Giuliani clearly is the victim of selective suspension based on the political content of his public speech, rather than on neutral principles.

When I came of age in the 1950s, there were many such selective suspensions and disbarments of attorneys. Back then the victims were largely radical left-wing lawyers—communists, former communists, and "fellow travelers"—or, in the South, they were civil rights lawyers. Today the victims of selective enforcement are largely right-wing supporters of former president Trump. The dangers to civil liberties and constitutional rights are similar in each instance.

Whether one is a liberal or a conservative, a Democrat or a Republican, everyone should be concerned when any lawyer—whether one approves or disapproves of their conduct—is suspended without a hearing based on vague criteria that curtail freedom of speech. As a liberal Democrat who voted for President Biden and who believes his election was fair and legitimate, I strongly disagree with the decision in the Giuliani case.

The Indictment of Navarro Is Unconstitutional

The indictment of Peter Navarro for contempt of Congress violates several provisions of the Constitution and should be dismissed. Navarro has a strong claim of executive privilege that should be decided by the courts before any indictment can lawfully be issued.

Either the Justice Department or Congress should seek a judicial ruling that Navarro's claim of executive privilege is invalid. If the court rules that it is invalid and orders him to respond to the congressional subpoena, Navarro should have an opportunity to comply. If he fails to comply with a judicial order, he can either be indicted or held in contempt by the court. But absent a judicial order, he cannot lawfully be indicted for invoking executive privilege and refusing to reveal arguably privileged material just because a committee of Congress, controlled by Democrats, has voted that he should. It is not enough to allow him to appeal after the fact, because information once revealed cannot be erased. He is obliged to claim privilege now and refuse to respond. That is not a crime. It is the constitutionally correct action.

Navarro's indictment violates several key constitutional rights, including due process, fair warning, and executive privilege. It also violates the separation of powers under which the courts have the authority to resolve conflicts between the legislative and executive branches over claims of executive privilege in response to legislative subpoenas. Due process and fair warning require that these issues first be resolved by the courts before an indictment can be issued.

The Biden Justice Department knows the law, and it should not be acting lawlessly to make political points. The events of January 6, 2021 were wrong, and Congress has the right to investigate them and issue appropriate subpoenas, but they must comply with the Constitution. Legitimate ends do not justify illegitimate means and issuing an indictment of a former executive decision without first obtaining a judicial order is an illegitimate tactic.

So, Navarro should move to dismiss the indictment, and the court should grant his motion. But in an age of partisan law enforcement, it is far from certain that neutral justice will be done. Some courts, too, have been caught up in result-oriented injustice: because they are understandably so opposed to what happened on January 6 and so determined to assure it will never happen again, they are motivated to allow others or themselves to take shortcuts and deny due process and other rights to anyone allegedly complicit in these events. That is not the way the system is supposed work, and it is inconsistent with constitutional justice.

In our age of pervasive partisanship, too many judges peek out from under their blindfolds and rule differently based on the faces and political affiliations of the litigants. Every ruling and decision—whether by a judge or justice department official—must pass the "shoe on the other foot test." It must be the same regardless of face, name, race, ethnicity, religion, gender, or political affiliation. So, the question must be asked: would this justice department have indicted a Democratic former executive official who claimed executive privilege in response to a congressional subpoena. We may learn the answer when the Republicans control the House and issue subpoenas for officials in the Biden White House. I hope it doesn't come to that because two wrongs don't make a right. But it may, because a dangerous precedent established by one party in control is likely to be used by the other party when it gains control.

And indicting a former executive official who has claimed privilege without first securing a judicial ruling is a very dangerous precedent. It is dangerous not only to former government officials but to ordinary citizens. Consider a citizen who refused to answer congressional questions about conversations with her priest or medical doctor—or a lawyer who refused to disclose confidential information he received from a client. If this indictment is allowed to stand, these citizens too could be indicted before their claims of privilege were adjudicated by a court. A dangerous precedent indeed—to the rule of law, the Constitution, and the rights of all Americans.

Stone Indictment and Arrest Raises Serious Questions

The indictment of former Donald Trump associate Roger Stone follows a long pattern that should raise serious concerns about the former special counsel. Like virtually all of these indictments, this one does not charge any major crimes relating to Russia that were committed before the special counsel was appointed. It charges crimes that grew out of the investigation and were allegedly committed after Robert Mueller was appointed in 2017.

Recall that the primary job of the special counsel was to uncover crimes that had already occurred relating to Russian involvement in the 2016 election. Mueller also was authorized to investigate and prosecute crimes growing out of the investigation, such as perjury and obstruction of justice, but this role was secondary to the primary one. It turns out that the secondary role has produced many more indictments of Americans than the primary one. A review of all the indictments and guilty pleas secured by Mueller shows nearly all of them fall into three categories.

First are process crimes such as perjury, obstruction, false statements, and witness tampering that have resulted from the investigation itself. That does not make them any less serious, but it is relevant to evaluating the overall success or failure of the primary mission. Second are crimes that occurred before Mueller was appointed but that cover unrelated business activities by Trump associates. The object of these indictments is to pressure the defendants to provide evidence against Trump. Third is one indictment against Russian individuals who will never be brought to justice in the United States. This indictment was largely for show.

The strategy used by the special counsel, as described by Judge T. S. Ellis III, is to find crimes committed by Trump associates and to indict them in order to pressure them to cooperate. This is what Ellis said about the indictment of Trump campaign chairman Paul Manafort: "You don't really care about Mr. Manafort's bank fraud. What you really care about is what information Mr. Manafort could give you that would reflect on Mr. Trump or lead to his prosecution or impeachment."

Ellis also pointed out the dangers of this tactic: "This vernacular to sing is what prosecutors use. What you have to be careful of is that they may not only sing, but they may also compose." This is indeed a tactic widely employed by prosecutors, particularly in organized crime and other hierarchical cases. However, the fact that it is common does not make this tactic right. "Civil libertarians have long expressed concern about indicting someone for the purpose of getting the individual to cooperate against the real target.

I have been writing about this issue for decades. In fact, I coined the term "compose" that Ellis cited in federal court. However, most fair-weather civil libertarians have remained silent with regard to Mueller because his target is Trump, who they despise. The American Civil Liberties Union, which has been flush with cash since Trump was elected, has expressed little criticism of the questionable tactics used by the special counsel.

It seems rather clear that the manner by which Stone was arrested, in an early morning raid on his home in Florida publicized by the media, was intended to apply pressure on him to cooperate. Ordinarily, a white-collar defendant would be allowed to surrender to authorities, unless there is fear of escape, which does not appear to be the case here, as evidenced by his low bail. Whether Stone "sings" or "composes" remains to be seen.

Stone has declared that he would never cooperate, but attorney Michael Cohen said he would take a bullet for Trump before he turned against him in an effort to get a reduced sentence. Prosecutors have many weapons at their disposal to get reluctant witnesses to cooperate, such as threatening to indict family members, as in the Michael Flynn case. Civil libertarians should be concerned about the tactics that are being used by Mueller to get witnesses to sing. All Americans should be concerned about the "ends justify the means" path taken by the special counsel.

Mueller came up largely empty on substantive crimes relating to Russia that were committed before he was appointed; he can point to the three categories of alleged crimes described above. It is difficult to declare his investigation a success, or his appointment justified by the results. Based on what we have seen, it would have been far better if a nonpartisan commission of experts had been appointed to investigate Russian involvement in the 2016 election and to make recommendations about how to prevent foreign interference in future American elections.

Is the New York Attorney General Selectively Going after the NRA?

The announcement that the Attorney General of New York is investigating the National Rifle Association and looking to shut it down raises serious constitutional concerns. I am no fan of the NRA. Politically, I think it wields too much influence against reasonable gun control, which I support as consistent with the Second Amendment. It is too closely connected

with the profitability of gun manufacturers. It advocates positions and supports candidates, even if indirectly, that I believe
undercut our safety. I will never contribute to the NRA, and I
will generally vote against candidates it supports. But to paraphrase Voltaire, I will strongly defend its right to be wrong.
The NRA is entitled under the First Amendment, to advocate
these views and to petition the government for what it regards
as a redress of grievances under the Second Amendment.

To be sure, the attorney general of New York has the
legitimate authority to investigate <u>all</u> eleemosynary (that is,
charitable) organizations that operate in New York. The key
word is <u>all</u>. If the attorney general of New York is applying
precisely the same standards of investigation to the NRA as
it applies to <u>all</u> other charitable groups that advocate controversial positions, including liberal and radical ones, then
I could not complain about unequal application of the law.
But I seriously doubt that the liberal Democrat who currently
holds the position of New York attorney general has investigated liberal charities with the same vigor that she is going
after the conservative NRA. In today's highly politicized
atmosphere, the burden is on her to demonstrate equal application of the law to all similarly situated charities, regardless
of their political positions. She has not satisfied that burden.

The apparently selective investigation of the NRA is part
of a larger problem: the weaponization of our justice system
for partisan and ideological purposes. The justice system
must always be above partisan politics. It cannot serve as a
weapon for either side in the political wars that are being
fought by both sides at this highly divisive time.

Again, to paraphrase, this time the Romans: "Who will
guard the guardians?" Who is investigating the decision by

the attorney general of New York to go after the NRA? Is
the media seeking her records of prior investigations of other
groups whose leaders may have used charitable contributions
for private or mixed charitable-private expenditures? Are
there governing standards for conducting such investigations? Or does the attorney general claim the power to pick
and choose which charitable organizations to investigate?

Today it is the liberal attorney general investigating the
conservative NRA. Tomorrow it may be a conservative attorney general investigating Planned Parenthood, the ACLU,
or anti-gun organizations. Does this investigation pass the "a
shoe on the other foot" test?

These and other questions should be addressed by the
media, by lawyer's groups in New York, and by others interested in the equal application of the law.

It would be a mistake for the NRA to pack up its bags
and move to Texas, as President Trump has suggested. If it is
being singled out because of its political positions, it should
stay and fight. Under the so called "castle doctrine" that
the NRA advocates, no one is required to leave their home
in the face of an intrusion (your home is your castle, hence
the term). I for one don't support a wide application of the
castle doctrine, but the NRA does. It would create a dangerous precedent if a politically motivated attorney general
could force a constitutionally protected advocacy group to
leave the state for fear of being selectively investigated.

No leaders of any charity have the right to cheat their
donors by spending contributions on personal, as distinguished from charitable, expenditures. The line between the
two is not always clear, especially when it comes to first class
travel and accommodations. But it is precisely because the

line isn't clear that objective standards equally applicable to all must be articulated and enforced. Absent such standards, the attorney general has too much discretion to use her considerable powers selectively and unfairly.

Applying uniform standards is particularly important when it comes to First Amendment–protected activity. Regardless of what anyone, including me, thinks of the NRA's politics, no one can doubt that its advocacy against reasonable gun control is core First Amendment activity that must be protected by the courts against selective investigations and efforts to shut it down.

Libraries Shouldn't Censor Trump Lawyer

Right-wing zealots have been trying to censor books they find objectionable in public libraries. There have been headlines such as 'Censorship Battles' New Frontier: Your Public Library; The American Library Association Opposes Widespread Efforts to Censor Books in US Schools and Libraries; and In a Lawsuit, a Group of Texas Library Patrons Says a Book Ban Amounts to Censorship.

But libraries do more than lend books. They sponsor speakers. Now, at least one public library is banning a speaker based entirely on partisan and ideological factors. I'm not talking about a Drag Queen Story Hour getting canceled. This time, a speaker is being banned by left-wing censors because, though a liberal all his life, he also once represented former president Donald Trump.

I wish I could write about this important free speech issue without getting personal. But the banned speaker is me and the library is my beloved local library in Chilmark, where I have spent nearly a half-century of long summers.

For years, I was the most popular speaker in a weekly series sponsored by my library, discussing subjects ranging from Thomas Jefferson to freedom of speech to Israel. The questions following my presentations would be contentious, intelligent, and thought-provoking. But once I began opposing then-president Trump's impeachment on the ground that he was not being charged with a constitutionally authorized offense, the library suddenly claimed that I was too popular and the crowds I attracted were too large.

So instead of simply limiting the audience, they decided not to invite me to give my usual annual lecture. Since that time, despite repeated requests by me and others, they have not permitted me to speak. More importantly, they have not permitted those residents of Chilmark who wanted to listen to my views to hear them at their library.

The claim that I attracted too large an audience was an obvious pretext. It reminds me of what Yogi Berra once said about a popular restaurant: "Nobody goes there anymore. It's too crowded." If I had supported Trump's impeachment, I would have been invited back every year.

Libraries are obviously allowed to exercise discretion, inviting who they wish. But in this case, my disinvitation was caused solely by the fact that I defended a president they didn't like. The fact that I voted against him twice didn't excuse my political sin.

To put this matter in a constitutional context, assume that a public, tax-supported small town Texas library decided to limit its speakers only to white supremacists or only to Trump supporters: Would such a restriction be constitutional? Wouldn't liberals and leftists be up in arms about using taxpayer money to promote one point of view while censoring another? Of course they would. What if the library turned down a liberal speaker who wanted to oppose white supremacy on the ground that his audience would be too large? Would anyone take that claim seriously?

I love public libraries. Much of my high school education took place at the Brooklyn Public Library's main branch at Grand Army Plaza. I was honored several years ago by that library for my public support of libraries. When I spoke at the Chilmark library, I always praised it and contributed the proceeds from book sales to the library.

My family and friends in Chilmark do not want me to sue the library. "It's too close to home," says one. "It's a local treasure," says another. I understand these concerns, I also know that if the local library were in the hands of pro-Trump conservatives, these same people would be encouraging me to sue it.

I have always lived my life on the basis of important principles, including freedom of speech and due process. Should I not seek to apply those principles to my own public library? If I don't, will the precedent be used to ban more liberal speakers in conservative parts of the country?

I can't accept the double standard. I don't want to sue my beloved library. I have offered the library several alternatives: limit the number of audience members; hold the event outdoors; have it in June or September when there are fewer people in Chilmark.

Thus far, the library has not accepted any of these reasonable alternatives. They apparently don't want to sponsor a speech by someone who defended the most hated man in Chilmark: Donald Trump.

The residents of Chilmark have a perfect right to disinvite me from parties, private concerts, and even fundraisers for the Jewish Democratic Council of America (as they recently did). But tax-supported public libraries are different. Their members have the right to listen to speakers they choose to hear.

Allowing the Chilmark library to select its speakers based on partisan considerations violates the spirit if not the letter of the First Amendment. It does not serve the interests of Chilmark residents who want to hear me. They may be few in number these days, but that only makes the excuse offered by the library even more absurd. The reality is that some prominent supporters of the library don't want my views to be sponsored by their library. And they have been given a veto over points of view and speakers that offend them.

Recently a sign was posted in Oak Bluffs, another town on Martha's Vineyard that read: "O. B. Welcomes Alan Dershowitz & FREE SPEECH."

So maybe I will be invited to speak there.

I hope we can resolve this issue in a win-win fashion. I don't want to sue the library, but I don't want to allow a precedent to stand under which libraries get to decide which speakers their constituents should hear. The next step will be deciding which books their constituents can read based on partisan considerations rather than readers' interests. In fact, the Chilmark Library, which included twenty of my books before I defended Trump, stopped lending any of the books I wrote after I defended him. When I learned about this censorship, I donated my new books to them so that readers could borrow them. I hope they make them available.

I Will Defend Any Lawyer Targeted by McCarthyist "65 Project"

A group of anti-Trump lawyers, calling themselves the "65 Project," has banded together to try to discipline, shame, and otherwise destroy the careers of 111 lawyers who filed sixty-five briefs—hence the name—seeking to overturn the 2020 election.

As a believer in the accuracy of the 2020 election, and as a Democratic supporter of Joe Biden, I thoroughly disapproved, as a matter of policy, of most of these efforts to overturn the election. But I disapprove even more thoroughly of efforts to attack the lawyers who filed these briefs.

The project is headed by zealous hard-left Democrats, though it includes several moderate Republicans and some well-intentioned lawyers. But their goals, as described by their supporters, are indecent to the core.

As one put it: "This is mostly important for the deterrent effect it can bring so you can kill the pool of legal talent going forward." One of its leaders also said that its purpose was to "shame them and make them toxic in their communities and in their firms." He acknowledged that "the little fish are probably more vulnerable to what we are doing ... threatening their livelihood ... [and] their reputations in their communities."

This is not the first time that groups of lawyers have tried to destroy the careers of other lawyers who have filed lawsuits with which they disagree.

During the 1950s McCarthy Era, several legal groups sought to destroy the reputations and careers of lawyers who defended the rights of accused Communists. During the civil rights movement of the 1960s, several southern legal groups tried to do the same thing to lawyers who were trying to dismantle segregation.

But this is the first time in my memory that centrists, liberals and leftists have organized to attack lawyers for filing legal briefs of which they disapprove.

McCarthyism of the left has become a serious problem throughout America. People are being fired, canceled, and shamed for expressing views that are not politically correct to progressives, wokes, and radicals. The formation of the 65 Project is among the most dangerous manifestations of this new form of left-wing McCarthyism.

I was not among the group of lawyers who were originally targeted, but I immediately offered my help to those lawyers who were, despite my strong disagreement with the substance of their lawsuits. To paraphrase a statement attributed to Voltaire: I fundamentally disagree with legal efforts to overturn the 2020 election, but I will defend the rights of lawyers who did so against McCarthyite attacks.

The implications of this new McCarthyism are frightening. It was only twenty-two years ago when lawyers like me sought to block the election of President George W. Bush, believing as we did that Al Gore actually received more votes than Bush in Florida and was the rightful winner. We lost in court. But back then no one suggested going after the hundreds of lawyers who tried to prevent Bush's certification. A dangerous weapon, like the 65 Project, unleashed by Democrats, will surely be used by Republicans at some future time.

There are remedies in place for lawyers who file briefs that are frivolous as a matter of law. The courts are equipped to deal with such lawyers and do not need the help of this highly toxic project, whose goal is to deter lawyers from using the courts to undo elections.

As a nation committed to the rule of law, we should be encouraging legal remedies in court, rather than violent responses on the streets. Some lawyers will inevitably go too far, as many have done in other contexts. But to establish a special project designed to intimidate lawyers from engaging in such election challenges is contemptible.

So, I invite other like-minded civil libertarians, who may disagree with the efforts to overturn the 2020 election, but who definitely disagree with efforts to cancel lawyers who believed otherwise, to join me in a nonpartisan civil liberties defense against this McCarthyite tactic.

[Following the publication of this op-ed, the 65 Project filed a bar complaint against me, despite the fact that I have never challenged the results of any 2020 or 2022 election. The only result I ever challenged was in the 2000 election of George Bush over Al Gore. (See *Supreme Injustice: How the High Court Hijacked Election 2000*.) I'm sure the members of the 65 Project approved of my challenge to that election.]

Why I Joined Mike Lindell's Legal Team

I disagree with My Pillow founder Mike Lindell about a lot of things, including his belief that the 2020 election was stolen from Donald Trump. I'm a liberal Democrat; he is a conservative Republican. Yet I am enthusiastically representing him in his lawsuit against the Justice Department and Federal Bureau of Investigation over the recent search and seizure of his telephone.

As soon as it was announced that I would be joining his defense team, people asked why I would be representing somebody they believe is trying to destroy American democracy. It's a good question.

It is important for Democrats who support Joe Biden's legitimate presidency and object to Mr. Trump's violations of constitutional norms to resist unconstitutional efforts by Mr. Biden's administration and supporters to abuse the law, particularly the criminal-justice system, against our political opponents. It is easy for Republicans to criticize the Justice Department for overreaching, just as it was easy for Democrats to criticize the Trump administration. What is difficult is to criticize officials of one's own party when they go too far. Yet it's essential to keep politics out of the justice system—for principled Democrats and Republicans alike to advocate strict compliance with constitutional norms, regardless of whose ox is being gored. This principled attitude was exemplified by Republican leaders who condemned Mr. Trump for his dangerous electoral shenanigans. Democrats should follow their example.

In my view as a longtime civil libertarian, the Justice Department went too far in seeking a search warrant against Mr. Trump's property at Mar-a-Lago. It could have asked the court to enforce the subpoena it issued and taken other less intrusive measures. It was also wrong in opposing a special master and demanding that the department's own lawyers be the only ones to determine whether privileged material was seized.

I also believe the department exceeded its constitutional authority by seeking and executing a search warrant against Mr. Lindell's telephone, which gives investigators access to his computer files and other private and business data. The Framers of the Constitution abhorred the British practice of issuing general warrants, which empowered the government to search entire homes and businesses. The seizure and search of a cellphone in today's connected world is more of a general search than rummaging through a home. Your entire life is stored on electronic devices.

Although the warrant in the Lindell case specified files that could be searched, it didn't specify a protocol for separating the searchable from the private and privileged, thus leaving it to the discretion of Justice Department officials to make these constitutionally critical determinations. This is why we seek judicial relief, including the appointment of a special master and an injunction against Justice Department lawyers now combing through Mr. Lindell's files. We are also trying to unseal the affidavit that accompanied the warrant request and to learn whether the FBI found Mr. Lindell at a Hardee's restaurant in Mankato, Minnesota, via electronic surveillance performed with a warrant.

The power of the government to surveil and search its citizens shouldn't be an issue that separates Democrats from Republicans or liberals from conservatives. All Americans should be concerned about limiting the power of the government. Tragically, we live in an age when partisanship determines which side of an important constitutional issue most people take.

If the Trump administration had done to a prominent Democratic supporter precisely what the Biden administration has done to Mr. Lindell, many Democrats would be outraged and support judicial relief. But today, few Democratic lawyers will represent Trump Republicans whose constitutional rights have been violated. This is a tragedy that endangers the neutrality of our Constitution and the legal profession. I will continue to defend the Constitution equally on behalf of Democrats and Republicans.

CHAPTER 3

Sacrificing Civil Liberties to Get Trump

M any Democrats who have claimed the mantle of civil libertarian have advocated anti–civil liberties tactics to prevent Trump from running again. I have tried to expose their hypocrisy in my op-eds.

The Importance of Upholding the Right to Counsel

Sometimes it takes an absurd event to explain the high cost of living a principled life. For nearly sixty years I have tried to emulate John Adams, Abraham Lincoln, Clarence Darrow, Thurgood Marshall, Edward Bennet Williams, and others in the pantheon of my legal heroes, by representing as they did, the most hated and vilified defendants. In making that career choice, I knew that I would be criticized by those who do not understand the constitutional right to counsel and the need for every defendant to receive zealous representation.

But when law professors such as Cornell's Michael Dorf—who is an acolyte, water carrier, and coauthor of America's most prominent constitutional hypocrite, Professor Laurence Tribe—set out to defame me for my principled representation of unpopular defendants, I realized how much trouble the Constitution is in. Dorf conducted what he called a "highly unscientific Twitter poll for the most embarrassing Yale Law School alum." He put my name prominently on the list because "Dershowitz, seems to take special pride in defending people whose alleged conduct he claims to disapprove—including especially, Donald Trump." (He apparently doesn't remember Voltaire's "I disapprove of what you say, but I will defend to the death your right to say it.") Dorf acknowledges that some people dislike me because "they disagree with his extreme conception of the lawyer as a zealous advocate." But he then goes on to say that I deserve special condemnation because I "represent men who behave terribly toward women (e.g., Claus von Bülow, O. J. Simpson, Mike Tyson, Jeffrey Epstein, Donald Trump) that suggests at least the possibility of misogyny." In his malice, he could not resist the temptation to make a veiled reference to the fact I once received a massage from a professional therapist in Jeffrey Epstein's home, years before I represented Epstein. He omitted the facts, detailed in my book *Guilt by Accusation*, that it was a shoulder massage and that my wife also received a massage, and that I never even met the woman who falsely accused me of having sex with her years after that therapeutic massage—a woman who has now recognized that she may have "made a mistake in identifying" me as someone with whom she had sex.

In purporting to describe my "career-long oeuvre of defending men," Dorf also maliciously omits the fact that I have defended more women than most other lawyers, including Mia Farrow, Patricia Hearst, Leona Helmsley, Lucille Miller, Sandra Murphy, and numerous less well-known women who alleged harassment by men. He also deliberately omits the fact that my "oeuvre" includes representing half of my clients on a pro bono basis and that many of my cases have focused on the First Amendment, the Fourth Amendment, and the death penalty. In light of Dorf's deliberately skewed presentation of my oeuvre, it is not surprising that I came out ahead of Justice Alito and even Stuart Rhodes (the founder of "Oath Keepers") in the left-wing unpopularity poll.

Normally I would ignore such a childish and malicious enterprise, because I have no idea how many people were included in his "unscientific pole," and how they were selected. (He acknowledges that the poll was "lawyer-skewed" and "liberal-skewed.") But the fact that so many highly educated people are prepared to condemn a lawyer for his oeuvre tells us something about today's legal education that cannot be ignored.

So, I will take my victory in Dorf's dishonor roll, as a red badge of courage, and I will continue to represent people he and his readers despise. I am proud to have gone to Yale Law School and to be living a life of principle based on what I was taught there by professors such as Alex Bickel, Telford Taylor, Joseph and Abe Goldstein, Jay Katz, and Guido Calabrese. I don't think they would be embarrassed by my oeuvre. They understood the crucial role of a zealous lawyer in our adversary system of justice. More important, they understood the alternative system that prevails in so many tyrannies, where zealous advocates and their unpopular clients are treated much worse than finishing atop Dorf's unpopularity poll.

Requiem for the American Civil Liberties Union

In a long and detailed article—really, an obituary—the *New York Times* announced the death of the American Civil Liberties Union (ACLU) as the primary defender of free speech in the United States. More than a century old, the ACLU was founded primarily to defend the free speech and due process of all Americans regardless of their views, party affiliation, race, or ideology.

The ACLU has defended Nazis, the KKK, pornographers, and purveyors of hate speech. I was privileged to serve on the national board of the ACLU during its golden age.

Then everything changed. The board decided to "diversify." This meant that a certain number of women, African Americans, Latinos, and gays had to be represented—which, in turn, meant the representatives of these groups were expected to prioritize the parochial interests of the groups they represented over the more general interests of all Americans pertaining to free speech and due process.

Unsurprisingly, the organization stopped prioritizing free speech and due process. Instead, it began to prioritize a woman's right to choose, gay marriage, racial issues, and "progressive politics." This trend began well before the election of President Donald Trump, but it came to a head when he took office. The ACLU turned into a money-making machine by prioritizing the anti-Trump attitudes of its new members over its traditional role as a nonpartisan defender of free speech and due process.

The ACLU is now rolling in money, but it is intellectually bankrupt in its defense of free speech and due process—especially when these core liberties conflict with its money-making progressive agenda. This is particularly true with respect to the attacks on free speech and due process on university campuses, which are rampant and largely ignored by the current ACLU.

The *Times* article documents the gradual death of a once-great and important organization and its transformation into yet another hard-left progressive advocacy group. But the *Times* missed the big story, because the big story is that what has happened to the ACLU is merely a symptom of what is happening throughout America. An equally important symptom is what has happened at the *New York Times* itself. Don't expect to see Michael Powell, the *Times* writer who penned the ACLU piece, write an equally explosive article about the demise of the *New York Times* as an objective newspaper of record. Young readers may not even know that the *Times* used to report all the news fit to print, rather than skewing the news to fit a progressive political agenda.

The young people who have destroyed the ACLU were educated—or miseducated—at the same institutions whose graduates now fill the newsroom of the *New York Times*. So the story of the ACLU is the story of the *New York Times* and is also the story of CNN, *The Washington Post*, *HuffPost*, Facebook, Twitter, and Google. It is the story of liberalism in America dying and being replaced by a radical progressive agenda that cares little about free speech, due process, or other civil liberties. These young lawyers, journalists, and editors know "The Truth" and see little need for dissenting opinions, due process, and other cumbersome mechanisms that stand between them and their hard-left utopia.

These young professionals don't understand that without basic civil liberties, every would-be utopia becomes a dystopia. They don't understand what the great Justice Louis Brandeis said a century ago: "The greatest dangers to liberty lurk in insidious encroachment by men of zeal, well-meaning but without understanding." Nor do they understand the equally important words of the great jurist, Judge Learned Hand: "The spirit of liberty is the spirit which is not too sure that it is right; the spirit of liberty is the spirit which seeks to understand the minds of other men and women; the spirit of liberty is the spirit which weighs their interests alongside its own without bias."

The death of the ACLU, along with the weakening of liberalism and our civil liberties, is among the most dangerous developments we now confront. As the founder of the ACLU cautioned nearly a century ago: "The struggle for liberty never stays won." We are now losing that battle, in no small part because the new leaders of the newly wealthy organization he founded have sold out and abandoned its original mission to defend the free speech and due process of everyone.

Double Standard: The ACLU

Civil liberties require a single standard without regard to party, ideology, or person. The right of Nazis to free speech must be protected with the same vigor as the right of Salman Rushdie. The ACLU in particular, and good civil libertarians in general, used to live by that creed. That's what makes them different from special pleaders for those who agree or identify with them. This great tradition—that led John Adams to defend the hated British soldiers who were accused of the Boston massacre and led the old ACLU to defend the right of Nazis to march through Skokie—has not been evident when it comes to Donald Trump. This double standard has been manifested in a number of ways.

The most serious alleged crime cited in the Trump search warrant is under the Espionage Act of 1917. In the past, many leftists and civil libertarians have railed against the breadth and scope of this law, calling it repressive and unconstitutionally vague. Among the people who were prosecuted, indicted, or investigated under the Espionage Act are progressive icons such as socialists Eugene V. Debs and Charles Shenk, antiwar activists Daniel Ellsberg and Dr. Benjamin Spock, whistleblowers Julian Assange and Chelsea Manning, anarchists Emma Goldman and Alexander Berkman, as well as many others who made unpopular speeches, engaged in protests, or took other actions deemed unpatriotic by the government. But now that the shoe is on the other foot—now that the same law is being deployed against a possible presidential candidate they deplore—many of these same leftists are demanding that this accordion-like law be expanded to fit Trump's alleged mishandling of classified material. The American Civil Liberties Union, which has repeatedly challenged the constitutionality and applicability of the espionage to anti-government activities by left-wing radicals, is strangely silent when the same overbroad law is deployed against a political figure whose politics they deplore.

The same double standard seems to be at work with regard to the search of Mar-a-Lago. Many civil libertarians have complained about the overuse of search warrants in situations where a less intrusive and narrower subpoena would suffice. Even Attorney General Garland acknowledged that the policy of the Justice Department is to use measures less intrusive than a full-blown search whenever possible. Yet he did not explain why a day-long search of Trump's home was necessary, especially since a subpoena had been issued and could have been judicially enforced if the government was dissatisfied with the progress of negotiations. Again, silence from the ACLU and other left-wing civil libertarians.

Then there is the manner by which Trump loyalists have been treated when they were indicted. They have been arrested, handcuffed, and shackled, despite not having been charged with crimes of violence and despite the absence of evidence that they were planning to flee. In my long experience, most other comparable defendants are simply notified of the charges and ordered to appear in court. Yet despite this apparent double standard, the left has been silent.

Attorney General Garland commendably stated that the Justice Department is dedicated to equal justice for all. But recent applications of the law suggest otherwise. "Due process for me but not for thee" seems to have replaced the equal protection of the law as the guiding principle.

Perhaps the most glaring manifestation of the double standard currently at work is the different approach taken to the alleged mishandling of classified material by Trump, on the one hand, and former presidential candidate Hillary Clinton, on the other hand. No search warrants were sought for Clinton's home where private servers were apparently kept. And then FBI director James Comey announced that no criminal prosecution has ever been taken for comparable mishandling of classified material. The same was true of former national security adviser Sandy Berger's deliberate hiding of such material in his socks. Berger was fined for willfully violating the law with regard to secret documents. Yet the espionage act was not invoked against him.

Equal justice for Democrats and Republicans must not only be done; it must be seen to be done. There must be one law—and one application of law—for all comparable acts and persons. There must also be one standard of civil liberties—and complaints about their violation—by principled civil libertarians. The salutary goal seems to be missing from recent attempts to get Trump and his loyalists regardless of the principle of equal justice for friend and foe alike.

To the contrary, those of us who—despite our opposition to Trump politically—insist that the same standards of civil liberties must be applied to him as to those we support politically, have lost friends, been defamed by the media, and been canceled. This unacceptable double standard is so widespread that it endangers the rule of law and the historic role of neutral, non-partisan civil liberties that protect it from partisan weaponization.

In Defense of "Whataboutism"

Following the raid on former president Trump's home, Hillary Clinton was seen sporting a baseball cap with the logo "But her emails." Hillary's hat is intended to mock the argument made by Trump supporters and some civil libertarians that the investigation of Trump's alleged security breaches must be evaluated against the way in which similar breaches by Hillary herself and by the late former national security adviser Sandy Berger, we're handled. Both were accused of mishandling confidential material. Berger was fined, and

Clinton was rebuked by former FBI director James Comey, which may have cost her the election. But neither was subjected to search warrants or espionage prosecution. Hence, the argument "but her emails."

This so-called argument has come to be called "whataboutism." Its implicit thesis is that every case should be judged on its merits and comparisons to other cases are beside the point. But apt comparisons are the point in a democratic society with a Constitution guaranteeing the equal protection of the laws. The way in which Clinton and Berger were treated is highly relevant in determining whether Trump is being subjected to a double standard of justice. The facts, especially the comparable degrees of culpability, may be different; and if so, that would provide a good answer to a whataboutism argument.

But if the facts are similar and the treatment is different, Americans are entitled to ask why. The shoe must fit comfortably on the other foot if justice is to be done and seen to be done. There cannot be one rule for Democrats and another for Republicans.

So, it is appropriate to ask the question, what about Clinton's emails? And what about Berger's attempt to hide classified materials in his socks? Mocking that question by wearing a hat with the slogan "but her emails" does not provide an adequate answer. Neither does the cliche "two wrongs do not make a right." The second wrong does not justify or excuse the first wrong, but unequal treatment of two comparable wrongs should raise concerns about fairness and equality. Two equal wrongs that are treated differently may make a third wrong!

Whataboutism may have a role to play in a limited number of cases. Perhaps presidents should be treated differently. It is often argued that presidents are not above the law, but neither are they below the law. When unequal treatment is shown, the burden shifts to those administering it to justify the inequality.

The questionable argument implicit in whataboutism is not new. There is a nineteenth-century Yiddish expression that says, "a for instance is not an argument." But sometimes it is. If a pattern of nonenforcement can be demonstrated, as with the Logan Act—an eighteenth-century law that forbids private citizens from negotiating with foreign countries—which has not been enforced in hundreds of years, it would be difficult to satisfy the burden of proving equal justice if it were to be suddenly and selectively invoked to target a political enemy. If, on the other hand, violation of the Classification or Records Acts were routinely prosecuted and alleged violators subject to a search warrant, then the case for equal application of the law will have been made.

Hillary Clinton should discard her hat. Just as Clinton's possible guilt does not excuse Trump's possible guilt, so too Trump's possible guilt does not excuse Clinton's. Her treatment of the emails and server were wrong, but not worthy of criminal prosecution. So may Trump's removal of possibly classified information. These two wrongs should encourage Congress to tighten up the laws regarding such information and the Justice Department to enforce them equally and fairly. But until they do, the "what about her email" argument should be taken seriously.

Should Biden Call MAGA Supporters Semi-Fascist?

President Joe Biden would have been correct had he accused some MAGA supporters of a totalitarian mindset that could lead to tyranny. But he was dead wrong in limiting this mindset to the hard right. It is at least equally applicable to many on the hard left. These so-called "progressives" are as opposed to freedom of speech and due process for thee, as are the extremists on the hard right. And it is the special obligation of liberals—like Biden and me—to focus at least as much attention on the dangers emanating from the hard left as those from the hard right.

Indeed, in some ways the totalitarian mindsets of many on the hard left are more dangerous than those of the hard right. The reason is that the hard left today is extremely influential on college and university campuses. Many hard left faculty members propagandize their students as to *what* to think instead of teaching them *how* to think for themselves.

These current students include our future leaders. In ten years, some will be in Congress, on editorial boards of major newspapers, in investment banks, and in other areas of enormous influence. In twenty years, one of them may be US president or another world leader, which is what the extremist leaders are counting on to achieve their goals.

So, the next time Biden decides to condemn what he calls semi-fascists of the hard right, he should spend at least as much time calling out the intolerant mindset of many of his own voters.

This is what President Joe Biden recently said about Trump MAGA supporters, according to *Politico*:

"What we're seeing now is either the beginning or the death knell of extreme MAGA philosophy," Biden told Democratic donors in the Washington suburb of Rockville. Calling out those he labeled as "extreme" Republicans, Biden said: "It's not just Trump, it's the entire philosophy that underpins the—I'm going to say something, it's like semi-fascism."

I generally disapprove of analogies between American politics and European fascism: the latter connotes Nazi Germany and fascist Italy. Thankfully, we are a long way from such tyrannies. Our constitutional system of checks and balances is designed to prevent any one branch of government from assuming dictatorial powers. It has worked for a quarter of a millennium and there is every reason to believe that it will continue to prevent the rise of dictators.

A better term would be "totalitarian mindset." It is certainly true that there are some extremists on both the "right" and the "left" who reflect an intolerant approach under which opposing views are seen to be unnecessary. Those who believe that they have the ultimate Truth on their side see no reason for allowing dissent from that truth, or for requiring due process before a person who they know to be guilty is convicted. Certainty is the essence of tyranny and skepticism is the enemy of tyranny.

Twitter: Musk Should Choose to Run Twitter Under the Spirit of the First Amendment

The widespread progressive reaction to Elon Musk's purchase of Twitter reflects a deep-seated fear of free speech by the hard

Left. NAACP president Derrick Jackson epitomized this fear when he proclaimed: "Mr. Musk, free speech is wonderful, hate speech is unacceptable. Disinformation, misinformation and hate speech have NO PLACE (caps in original) on Twitter." But who would get to define such "unacceptable" genres of speech? Well, naturally, Mr. Jackson and others of his political and ideological bent, who currently dominate much of social media and media in general. The desired result by Jackson and others on the hard Left would be "free speech for me, but not for thee."

The freedom to speak freely means the freedom to be wrong and to offend others. The marketplace of ideas should not include "safe" spaces for those who claim to be "harmed" by views with which they strongly disagree. It should include "rebuttal" spaces that permit the offended to reply with better arguments. The answer to "bad" speech is "better" speech that can prevail in the raucous marketplace of speech and counter-speech.

Freedom of speech is anything but free of social costs. It can be costly. It can cause hurt and harm. It can confuse and distort. But what is the alternative? A system that picks and chooses among "acceptable" forms of speech? What is hateful to one group may be acceptable to another. Moreover, banning some forms of unacceptable speech may be hateful to those who are banned. As Justice John Harlan put it in a case involving a man wearing an offensive jacket with the words "f*** the draft" spelled out: "One man's vulgarity is another man's lyric." There is no objective, neutral criteria for defining one person's or group's disinformation, misinformation, or hate speech. Such a determination is in the eye— or experience—of the beholder.

Those who fear Musk's proclaimed approach to openness on Twitter have proposed no reasonable alternatives. Selective censorship by invisible platonic guardians—such as currently exists in much of social media—is much worse. To paraphrase Churchill: Free speech may be the worst approach—except for all the others that have been tried over time.

To be sure, Twitter is not the government, so it is not bound by the First Amendment. It may censor if it chooses, but it may also choose not to censor. Several private universities have announced that they would comply with the spirit of the First Amendment, even though they are not bound by it. (Not all have done so, in practice.) That is what Twitter should do: announce that it will ban only material that would not be protected by the First Amendment if the government were to try to censor it.

The First Amendment does allow for some censorship, including direct incitement to violence, child pornography, and malicious defamation. But it does not allow censorship based on a singular definition of what is true or what is false. As Chief Justice William Rehnquist once put it: "Under the First Amendment, there is no such thing as a false idea." The Constitution leaves that to the marketplace. Twitter should follow that model.

There are several social media platforms that have come close to the principles of the First Amendment—including Rumble, on which my own podcast, "The Dershow," appears. I chose Rumble precisely because of its anti-censorship policies.

The end result of moving Twitter from its current selective censorship stance to a more free speech policy will result in some very bad things. There will be more hate speech, more misinformation, more personal attacks, and more garbage. That's why every social media platform has an off switch. If you don't like it, don't access it. But don't prevent others from doing so.

Freedom of speech is a dangerous experiment that our Founding Fathers undertook aware of its downsides, which have only gotten worse with the advent of pervasive social media. Elon Musk now has the ability to extend that dangerous experiment beyond the government to the giant provider of much of the information generated today. He has undertaken an enormous responsibility. Let us hope he bears it with the best interests of the world, which he will be serving with his ownership of this powerful tool.

Twitter: Why Is the Left So Afraid of Twitter?

A campaign is currently underway by left-wing organizations and politicians to demand that Twitter, now owned by Elon Musk, continue its practice of censoring hate speech and other "objectionable" postings.

A letter sent to Twitter's top twenty advertisers, signed by forty activist organizations, including the NAACP, the Center for American Progress, GLAAD, and the Global Project Against Hate and Extremism, contained the following veiled threat:

> We, the undersigned organizations call on you to notify Musk and publicly commit that you will cease all advertising on Twitter globally if he follows through on his plans to undermine brand safety and community standards, including gutting content moderation.

This means that Musk must not roll back what Twitter has on the books now and commit to enforcing the existing rules. In other words, Twitter advertisers have been asked to boycott Twitter unless it continues to censor.

Decades ago, during the height of McCarthyism, it was the hard right that demanded censorship, while the left insisted that the marketplace of ideas should be left open to all forms of speech.

As Thomas Jefferson wrote in 1801:

[W]e have nothing to fear from the demoralizing of some if others are left free to demonstrate their errors, and especially the law stands ready to punish the first criminal act produced by false reasoning. These are safer correctives than the conscience of a judge.

Jefferson's distrust of "the conscience of a judge" would probably be even greater if the censors were the CEOs of companies that rely on advertisers for their profits.

At a time of growing division, hostility, and violence, it is understandable to look to censorship as the easy solution to a difficult problem. But censorship requires censors, and once censors are given the ability to pick and choose what the public will hear, this slippery slope moves us away from freedom and toward repression.

I certainly do not like the kind of anti-Semitic hate speech that is pervasive on many of today's internet platforms, and I am the recipient of these emails and tweets on an almost daily basis. Free speech is not free.

The old expression that "sticks and stones may break my bones, but names will never hurt me" is false. Names hurt me, my family, and others. But that is not the issue. The issue is whether in an open society we must endure these pains to avoid being in even greater pains of selective censorship.

The Framers of the First Amendment chose to endure the pain of too much speech over the dangers of speech controlled by the government. But Twitter is not the government. Neither is Facebook or YouTube. They are giant media companies that dominate and control the flow of speech throughout the world. And the dangers of putting control of those flows in the hands of invisible elitist censors threatens to undercut our most important freedom.

This is the most important free speech issue that will be faced during the remainder of the twenty-first century: whether to tolerate untrammeled and sometimes even dangerous freedom of speech or to demand private censorship of the kind that the government could not impose.

Some have proposed that we treat giant social media companies like "common carriers," such as railroads and telegraph companies. But under the First Amendment, placing controls over public speech is different from regulating travel and even personal telegraph communications.

One manifestation of the divisiveness of our nation is that complex issues of this kind are rarely debated dispassionately and intelligently. Instead, people are forced to choose sides: are you for Musk or against him? Are you for controls on internet speech or against it?

The first casualty of divisive extremism is nuance. And it is nuance that is sorely needed with regard to this issue of internet censorship.

Let nuanced proposals be offered and discussed. Let us not rush to judgment about so important and complex issues.

And most important, let free speech not become weaponized as a partisan issue.

Following Musk's purchase of Twitter, it was disclosed that various government actors may have surreptitiously tried to encourage Twitter to censor some material. If this is true, it raises serious First Amendment and transparency issues worthy of further inquiry. There are differences, of course, between censorship—private or government—of scientifically proven, medically dangerous advice and political opinions. Musk was criticized for ending Twitter's COVID misinformation policy, and Musk himself misinformed his followers about COVID in March 2020, when he assured them that the US was likely to have "close to zero new cases" by the end of that April. He has also called for the prosecution of Dr. Anthony Fauci. These facts illustrate the dangers of placing censorship decisions in the hands of any one person.

CHAPTER 4

Will Trump Be Indicted?

———

The debate is raging about whether Donald Trump should and will be indicted. The *Wall Street Journal* conducted a lengthy interview with me on this and related topics. It is slightly edited for repetition and clarity. I also wrote about them in op-eds.

Wall Street Journal Interview

On the latest episode of *Free Expression*, constitutional lawyer Alan Dershowitz tells *Wall Street Journal* editor-at-large Gerry Baker the chances of an indictment for the former president are rising. But he says the aggressive approach by the Department of Justice and the FBI are undermining trust in American justice and explains why the hard left is the true danger to the future of democracy.

Gerry Baker: Hello, and welcome to *Free Expression* with me, Gerry Baker, editor-at-large of the *Wall Street Journal*. This week as Donald Trump's battle with the FBI and the justice department reaches a new intensity over the search of his Mar-a-Lago resort three weeks ago, I'm speaking with legal scholar and former Trump defender Alan Dershowitz. Professor Dershowitz is a constitutional lawyer and former professor of law at Harvard University. He was part of Donald Trump's defense team during the former president's first impeachment trial in 2020, though he points out that he is not a political supporter of Trump, in fact, describing himself as a Democrat and having voted for the president's opponents in the past. Professor Dershowitz has been a prominent figure in many criminal and constitutional cases over the years, and he's never been afraid to embrace controversy, or indeed, what some would deem even notorious causes and defendants. Among those he's defended have been O. J. Simpson, and perhaps most famously, Jeffrey Epstein. He's recently said he's become the latest victim of cancel culture as a result of his sometimes-controversial actions, saying he's been shunned by polite society. He's the author of many books. The latest of which is *The Price of Principle: Why Integrity Is Worth the Consequences*. And Alan Dershowitz joins me now. Alan, thank you very much for being here.

Alan Dershowitz: Thank you. I've been shunned by impolite society, not polite society, and not only have I been shunned, but the library in Chilmark has refused to allow me to speak after inviting me year after year. They initially did not carry any of the books I wrote since the time I defended the Constitution on behalf of Trump. And when the library starts restricting free speech, we know we have a problem.

Gerry Baker: Let's get straight onto this question of Trump now and his continuing battle with the FBI and the Justice Department. The very latest news was a late filing on Tuesday from the Justice Department in response to a motion from former president Trump who wants the appointment of a special master to review the documents. The Justice Department responded to that with a very lengthy and detailed account of its investigation, and indeed of the timeline of the investigation that's been going on over these documents that President Trump is alleged to have taken according to the Justice Department, perhaps unlawfully. I quote the *Wall Street Journal*'s reporting here today, "The efforts were likely taken to obstruct the government's investigation of documents at the former president's Mar-a-Lago home." Months before FBI agents searched the Florida state court filing late Tuesday, objecting to Mr. Johnson's proposal, laid out the government's most detailed timeline yet. And it said that there was likely evidence of obstruction by the president. What do you make of it? And what do you make of this fight that's going on?

Alan Dershowitz: The motion that is the basis for this dispute is a motion to have an independent non-justice department official review the possible lawyer-client privilege material that was seized pursuant to a search warrant. There are two things that are not in dispute. One, they seized some material that is subject to lawyer-client privilege. And number two, Justice Department officials have already reviewed that. That's wrong. When a lawyer and a client get together, and I know I've done this, what, a thousand times in my career, you make a promise that nobody will ever know what we spoke about. Certainly, the government will never know it. And yet the government claims, and they've been claiming for years, and I've been complaining about it for years, that they're entitled to have people in the Justice Department called a taint team, reviewing all these lawyer-client privileged secrets and deciding which are privileged, which are not, turning over the ones that are not privileged to the prosecuting team, but keeping secret the ones that are privileged from the prosecuting team. Let me just throw out this hypothetical. Let's assume that this taint team, these are prosecutors who have lunch with the prosecutors who are trying the case on a regular basis. Let's assume that this taint team discovers a letter or an email that is clearly covered by lawyer-client privilege. It starts out by saying lawyer-client privilege. This is a confidential communication. And in it, there is a smoking gun, or there is very, very juicy material about Donald Trump, which isn't criminal, but which could destroy his career. Does anybody in the United States actually believe that that material would remain totally secret and with a wink and a nod, its content wouldn't be communicated to fellow Justice Department officials? Would anybody ever speak to a lawyer in confidence again, if they knew that their conversation and communications would be reviewed by a Justice Department official? So, I think it's a very easy call to say, as some judges have previously said, that an independent master, a former judge, a former president of a university, somebody who has no connection with the Justice Department should be the one that is reviewing these privileged communications. And the only one to read what may be privileged communications and even the special master. As soon as he sees lawyer-client privilege, he should stop reading. And that should be the end of the matter. So, I think that the government is going about this all wrong. As far as obstruction of justice is concerned, let the chips fall where they may. I am not a Trump defender. I am a defender of the Constitution and the rule of law. If there is evidence of obstruction of justice, and it was legally obtained, and it's not covered by lawyer-client or executive privilege, my God, there should be a prosecution. I have no question about that. I haven't seen that so far in the unredacted affidavit, but if there is such evidence, the investigations should go forward. Obstruction of justice is a very serious charge.

Gerry Baker: So, what do you make of the Justice Department's response then to the Trump motion? This long document, again, which I said lays out a kind of a timeline essentially of the government's investigation, makes these allegations about obstruction of justice, including rather unusually a photograph I think of some of the documents that have been recovered so far with top secret sort of splashed all over them. Is this a smoke screen? Is it political? Is it for public consumption? Is it likely to have a dispositive effect on the judge, or do you think the judge is actually going to side with Trump and say actually for the reasons you've said these very concerning issues of lawyer-client privilege, that actually these documents do need to be reviewed by a special master before the Justice Department is allowed to get their hands on?

Alan Dershowitz: Well, it could cut both ways. If there is actual evidence of fraud, and if some of the lawyer-client conversations contained proof of fraud, there may be exceptions to the lawyer-client privilege. But what the government is doing is cherry picking what they want the public to see. They're redacting what they don't want the public to see. And some of the redactions may be fair. The names of agents, names of cooperating witnesses, but some of the redactions may be designed just to present a negative case against Trump without including the positive materials, if there are any positive materials. The question is really who you trust. Trust, but verify, as Reagan said. That's always been my philosophy. My job is not to trust the government. My job is to challenge the government at every turn and to make sure that it dots its i's and crosses its t's and operates within the rule of law and under the constitution. And we can't trust the Justice Department to guard itself. Who will guard the guardians? Goes back to Roman times, and it's reflected in our Constitution by our system of checks and balances. No department of government goes unchecked. Not the FBI and not the Justice Department.

Gerry Baker: We've plenty of reasons for the mistrust that we've seen over the last four or five years with regard to the way the Justice Department has behaved. I want to step back here and look at the broader case of the investigation here, which of course was initiated by the National Archives and Records Office over this dispute, which began, I mean, immediately after President Trump left office over which records he was allowed to keep. So, stepping back from these specific issues that have risen from these recent filings and motions, do they have a case there for pursuing the former president in this way?

Alan Dershowitz: Yes, they do. Remember 91 percent or something of people in the district voted against Trump. So yes, they have enough to start an investigation, but I think to go beyond an investigation, you have to satisfy two standards, particularly if you're going after a future potential presidential candidate against the incumbent president. It has to pass two standards. One, the Richard Nixon standard and the other, the Hillary Clinton standard. The Richard Nixon standard says you don't indict a president [or candidate] unless you have bipartisan support, unless there's a widespread consensus, unless Republican leaders also agree that there's a basis for indictment. That standard hasn't yet been met. The second standard and the one most relevant to your question is the Hillary Clinton standard. There's an old, great prayer in Passover: Why is this night different from every other night? And the question here is why is this case different from Hillary Clinton's case? She had material on her own server. It ended up on Wiener's computer, posing real dangers of being released. The government has a burden of demonstrating that this case was far, far more serious. Now, if the obstruction case holds up, that may satisfy both standards. After all, Nixon was guilty of obstruction of justice, and the evidence there was overwhelming and clear. If the evidence here becomes overwhelming and clear, then the Nixon standard might be satisfied. And the same thing would be true of the Clinton standard, because there was no claim of obstruction of justice there. She was cooperative. Let me be clear what's not obstruction of justice. And that is when the subpoena was issued, the lawyers fought it, and they fought it very hard, and they should fight it. I would've done the same thing if one of my clients was subpoenaed. So having a fight about a subpoena is not obstruction of justice. But destroying documents, obviously that are under subpoena, does constitute obstruction of justice. Of course, they were claims that happened in the Hillary Clinton case as well. And I don't know enough about that case to validate that, but certainly the right-wing media have talked a lot about destroying so many thousands of this and whitewashing that. I think that has to be looked at, because that standard also has to be met before a future presidential candidate is subject to criminal prosecution. You can't apply the law to your enemies when they're running against you politically, unless the case is overwhelming and clear.

Gerry Baker: Do you have to demonstrate that the president is somehow jeopardizing national security or just in breach of the presidential records act or whatever else it is? Does the Justice Department actually have to say, "Well, actually these are examples," obviously, without giving specifics, "but these are examples of the kinds of highly delicate national security information." Do you think they need to do that to make the case?

Alan Dershowitz: Well, you've asked a very, very good question. Defense lawyers have come up with a strategy called graymail in which what they say to the government is if you want to prosecute our guy on classified or secret information, you have to disclose the classified or secret information under the Sixth Amendment. We have a right to confront it and to contradict it. And the government says, "No, no, no, no. We don't want to disclose the classified information. That's why we brought this lawsuit." And a statute was passed, and court decisions have been rendered trying to strike an appropriate balance between the defendant's Sixth Amendment rights to confront evidence against him and the government's legitimate power to keep certain material classified. So, it's the beginning of a long process.

Gerry Baker: There is this defense that has been made by some of the Trump team. The president is the ultimate arbiter of classification in the United States. Obviously as the head of the executive branch, what he declares to be classified is classified, and what he declares to be not unclassified is presumably declassified. So, there are arguments about how exactly that declassification process work. Does he formally have to issue a memorandum or statement or whatever, a formal declaration of declassification, or can he just by his very act of taking a box out of the White House and shipping it down to Mar-a-Lago, does that in effect represent a de facto declassification? And therefore, is that the defense that Trump can say, I declassify these documents.

Alan Dershowitz: It surely will be the defense. I have no doubt about that. And it's partially legal defense and partially a factual defense. Let's start with the factual. It's clear that if the legal opinion is that the president can declassify, he can only declassify when he was president. And so, the argument would have to be that the very act on the last day in office, on January 20th, before noon of sending the boxes away, constituted an act of declassification. I don't think that would necessarily wash. Look, the law is not only terribly unclear on this, it's terribly wrong. The president should not have the independent authority to classify and declassify privately. It is alleged, and I don't know this to be the case, but I've heard it, that President Bush in the middle of a meeting in which certain material came up, announce that, okay, I'm going to declassify that right now so we can continue to have this conversation. There, of course, there was evidence of that. I don't think it has to be in writing, but the president, if he's going to declassify, it has to be while he's president. He cannot declassify retroactively after he gets a subpoena. So, this will be largely an issue of fact. Is there a memorandum in the files? Are there witnesses? It's a defense. Is it a strong defense? It depends on the evidence.

Gerry Baker: What about the issue of how sensitive these documents may be? That even if he had declassified them, there is the argument that the government has a legitimate interest, the Biden administration, the continuing government has a continuing interest in securing documents that could have vital national security implications. We don't know what's in these documents. It could be anything from Christmas cards from Kim Jong-un to names and places of intelligence agents inside the Chinese government. We're behind the veil of ignorance. But supposing it were the latter. Supposing there were documents in Mar-a-Lago there and among the tchotchkes and everything else that do have intelligence information that is vital to the national security of the United States. Is that something that they would say, "Look, irrespective of the president's rights to declassify, this is not a secure place. You know Mar-a-Lago, Alan, as well as anybody. It's not a secure place for secrets that are so vital of the security of the United States.

Alan Dershowitz: Well, first of all, there is not a complete veil of ignorance. We have dozens of years of experience with the government claiming that material was dangerous to the national security. I was one of the lawyers in the Pentagon Papers case. I represented Senator Mike Gravel, who read the Pentagon Papers into the congressional record. When that case was argued in front of the Supreme Court, the Solicitor General of the United States, the former Dean of the Harvard Law School, Irwin Griswold represented to the Supreme Court that if the Pentagon Papers were allowed to be published by the *New York Times* and the *Washington Post*, it would cause tremendous damage to the national security of the United States. The Pentagon Papers were published. And as far as I know, there was no damage to the national security. This has happened over and over and over and over again. The government cries wolf when it comes to national security. Materials are often classified to protect the personal and political interests of the people who are classifying, not the national security interests of the United States. And I would think that the *Wall Street Journal*, the *New York Times* would be at the forefront of arguing against over-classification. And they have in certain cases, but not so much in other cases. So, I do think that we have to look with suspicion and doubt on government's claims of high levels of national security. Now if there was material of national security, the government would've gotten a search warrant in February, and they would've acted on the search warrant the day they got it last month. They didn't do that. They waited a couple of days. The way to go is to subpoena the material. And that way, if you enforce the subpoena, the judge says, bring the boxes in tomorrow. At that point, the boxes are out of the control of Donald Trump. They are in the control of the court. Then a special master could be appointed to go through all the materials, see what's classified, see what's declassified. See what's lawyer-client privilege, see what's executive privilege, and the process would be orderly. But instead, they issued a search warrant in which they grabbed everything, including lawyer-client privileged materials, and according to reports at least, they went into Mrs. Trump's closet. It was overbroad. And so, yes, I take seriously claims of national security, but I have my own suspicion as to whether the government cries wolf too often when it comes to claims of national security.

Gerry Baker: We've seen a pretty remarkable inversion haven't we with media in the last sort of, I don't know, five, ten, fifteen years or whatever. When back in the sixties to seventies with the Pentagon Papers and Watergate, the newspaper reporter's kind of stance was to be deeply skeptical of the intelligence state and the law enforcement and the security state. But there are a lot of reporters who now seem to adopt a position of kind of deference, and indeed dare I say, kind of regard themselves as sort of vehicles for the intelligence state and for law enforcement.

Alan Dershowitz: You make that point very, very well. The current media does not pass the shoe on the other foot test. Would they be saying the same thing if this were an investigation of President Hillary Clinton, or even now of

President Biden. Take, for example, the Espionage Act of 1917, the worst civil liberties statute passed in the twentieth century. And according to many, the second worst civil liberty statute ever passed after the Alien and Sedition Acts. The *New York Times* and the ACLU have been railing against the Espionage Act of 1917. Now they want to expand it. They want to make it even more overarching and broad. So, what we're seeing is incredible hypocrisy, a failure of the shoe on the other foot test, a different standard for Trump than for other people. And by the way, it's not a Republican-Democrat divide. It's an anti-Trump pro-Trump divide. Now I'm one of the few people, I'm anti-Trump, but I put the Constitution way before any of my partisan interests. And I'm going to stick with the same approach I've taken for sixty years to the Espionage Act of 1917 to over-classification. I'm just not going to change my standards. And the reason I had to write my book, *The Price of Principle*, is because I haven't changed my standards. They want me to change my standards like the *New York Times* has. They want me to say Trump is different. If the object is to get Trump, the Constitution be damned, the First Amendment be damned, the Fourth Amendment be damned, the Sixth Amendment be damned. Get Trump. That is McCarthyism. I experienced McCarthyism in the 1950s. In that case, people said, get the communist. It doesn't matter what the cost is. Forget about the Constitution. In those days, it was Republicans saying that. Today, it's Democrats saying it.

Gerry Baker: What is it about Trump that has caused this? I mean, again, his detractors would say, "Well, it's because he does things that are at minimum, highly unorthodox, contrary to the norms of constitutional behavior." From the start, he has had a kind of fast and loose approach to the Constitution and to the truth and all this kind of stuff. His defenders would say it's just because he represents such a radical change and a radical threat to the "deep state and the establishment." What's your sense of why it is that he seems to have attracted this level of opprobrium. And in particular, to the point, as you say, where reporters will go to extraordinary lengths, including sitting sort of deferentially and uncritically, listening to Trump's opponents and critics in the government. What do you think it is?

Alan Dershowitz: It's largely Trump's fault. Trump has violated the norms of governance. Trump has done things that no president ought to do. Let's talk about the claim that he won the election. That's central. That was a fake claim. That was a dangerous, dangerous attack on our Constitution. It's utterly unjustifiable, and it should make everybody be very concerned about Trump. And I'm not here to defend any of that. I'm here to say that no matter how bad Trump has been, the ends do not justify the means. And you cannot go after him on unconstitutional grounds. Let's remember what communism was in the 1950s. China had gone to the Communist, Cuba, Eastern Europe. Khrushchev had said, "We'll bury you." There was a great danger of communism. It was a serious danger. It was way, way overstated. But the people on the right were genuinely afraid. And they said, "It's more important to stop communism than to defend the Constitution." People are saying the same thing now. I can tell you when Larry David confronted me on the porch of the Chilmark store and called me disgusting, because I had patted Mike Pompeo on the back congratulating my former student for what he had done in the Middle East. Larry really meant it. It was as if he was talking to Adolf Hitler's chief assistant, because I had defended President Trump. The veins in his forehead bulged. If you gave him a lie detector test, he would say, "This is the worst thing that's ever happened to America." So, I understand that, but I don't approve of even that justifying trashing the Constitution as Larry David and others want me to do. I won't do it.

Gerry Baker: The Archives Office do have these legitimate concerns and they are trying to recover these documents, they've been in these negotiations with Trump and Trump's lawyers for eighteen months now. They've recovered some of them. There's been some cooperation from Trump's people, maybe not enough, according to the government, but they've been trying to do this. They've got to a point they do seem to have got to an impasse where this latest filing that Trump people were telling them, there's no more documents. And in fact, were documents and all of this stuff, what other recourse did they have?

Alan Dershowitz: Very simple. You go to court immediately, and you enforce the subpoena. You get the judge to issue an order, demanding that Trump and his council turn all those boxes over now, within an hour. You can even enforce the subpoena by sending marshals to the place to make sure that the subpoena is enforced. The difference is the government doesn't get to look inside the boxes without the need for somebody independently to go through them and to decide what's privileged, what's not privileged, what's classified, what's not classified. Even Garland said in his statement that the justice department's policy is not to use a search warrant, unless there's no other less intrusive reasonable alternative. There was a simple, reasonable alternative here. Enforce the subpoena. They didn't want to do that, because subpoenas are not nearly as intrusive as search warrant. You couldn't get a subpoena to search Mrs. Trump's closet. Perhaps you couldn't get a subpoena to search the locked safe. You couldn't get a subpoena to look at lawyer-client privileged material through a taint team. So, the government gets a tremendous tactical advantage by using a search warrant, but there was an alternative and they failed to use it. So, my view is that there was probable cause for getting a search warrant. Don't blame Judge Reinhardt. There was probable cause, but search warrants are given out as easily as Halloween candy. The fault is with the Justice Department for seeking a search warrant. The same thing is true of an indictment. It would be easy for the government now to get an indictment based simply on the fact that there's classified material that's supposed to be in the Archives in the possession of the former president. They could get an indictment, but they should not seek one unless the criteria that I've laid out, the Nixon-Clinton criteria, are met. So, there's an enormous difference between what you can do and what you should do. Just because you can do it, doesn't mean you should do it.

Gerry Baker: Where does this go, Alan? Do you think there is going to be an indictment? That's going to be an actual prosecution?

Alan Dershowitz: Before yesterday I thought no, but with the latest filing and claims of obstruction of justice, I think the evidence is now tilting a little bit more toward the possibility of an indictment. If they can meet the Nixon standard. And you're right, by the way, the partisanship has grown great. But there are leaders of the Republican party who, if there was a clear case of obstruction of justice, a clear case of destruction of documents with no justification, I think there are Republican leaders who would say enough's enough. He's crossed that threshold.

Gerry Baker: And what's the charge? Is it obstruction of justice? Is it some offenses related to the Presidential Records Act?

Alan Dershowitz: Wouldn't be the Presidential Records Act. That would not satisfy the Clinton standards. It wouldn't satisfy the Berger standard. You can't use laws for the first time against a man who's about to run against your incumbent president. It has to be standard laws that have been enforced for many, many years against many people of both parties. That's why obstruction of justice is so important. If that can be proved, that would satisfy the standards.

Gerry Baker: And this would be obstruction of justice related to his demurral, his refusal to hand over the...

Alan Dershowitz: No, that wouldn't be enough. His refusal wouldn't be enough. That's not obstruction. You can deal with that through a subpoena. What would be obstruction is destroying documents, bribing. What Nixon did. He obstructed justice in the clearest sense of the word, offering bribes. There was no doubt about that. There would have to be a high level of willful and deliberate obstruction of justice for that charge to be brought.

Gerry Baker: And to be clear, you think they will make that charge?

Alan Dershowitz: I think it's tilted toward an indictment with the claims of obstruction of justice, that without the claims of obstruction of justice, I don't think they had any possible case for indictment. If they can make out a case for obstruction of justice, it then tilts toward the possibility of an indictment.

Gerry Baker: I'd like to talk about January 6th. There was some speculation early on in this process that maybe the government was actually kind of fishing to try and find some documents that might help them making a case that Donald Trump broke the law, and recommend to the Justice Department that they bring a prosecution. What's your sense of where all that is going in terms of Trump's potential legal jeopardy?

Alan Dershowitz: Well, first there's an enormous difference between doing the wrong thing and being criminally indicted. Trump did the wrong thing. He should never have made that speech on January 6th. It was constitutionally protected, but so are the Nazis marching through Skokie or communists. He should not have made that speech. It was a provocation. Yes, he used the words patriotically and peacefully, but if you look at the whole speech in context, it should not have been made, but it was constitutionally protected. It was not incitement. It was advocacy under the leading cases in the Supreme Court. Again, as usual, Trump's enemies are overstating the situation. Take for example, my former colleague Laurence Tribe, who on CNN announced that he thought that President Trump should be indicted for the attempted murder, the attempted murder of Vice President Pence. Now statements like that are so overblown that they hurt the credibility of the side making them. The same thing was true of the congressional committee. Foolishly, the congressional committee did not include any pro-Trump supporters. Two of them were proposed, Pelosi turned them down, and then the Republicans foolishly refused to put substitutes in. Therefore, there is no pro-Trump subpoena power, no pro-Trump cross-examination. And so, the committee itself lacked credibility. So, I don't think there will be a January 6th indictment. I'm not sure. I'm now representing one of the young men, a law school student who went to peacefully and patriotically protest and went into the Capitol and left when he was told to leave after having essentially been welcomed by waves by the police. And so, there are many, many such cases pending, but putting the criminal blame on the president for that will be a bridge too far.

Gerry Baker: Finally, I do want to talk a little bit about the broader climate that we have. You described your encounter with Larry David and the fact that you are barred from a library. Alan, you would acknowledge this; you have been a controversial figure, and you've embraced some controversial, indeed even notorious causes, and Jeffrey Epstein perhaps among the most striking.

Alan Dershowitz: I've never been in any way canceled for any of those things. People said, "You're like John Adams." You represented the Boston Massacre. You've represented the most heinous and the most seriously accused criminal. I've never, ever been canceled for that.

Gerry Baker: Essential part of our democracy that people, however heinous the crimes they may be accused of, are entitled to the best defense they can get. Right?

Alan Dershowitz: Yeah. I'll give you an example. Tomorrow's my 84th birthday. For my 80th birthday, we had a party on the deck of our Chilmark house in which close to a hundred people, neighbors, attended. This is after I defended Epstein. This is after I defended many of the other people. It was the defense of Donald Trump which turned everything around, which turned friends into enemies. The Trump factor is the most significant factor in creating the intolerant climate that we now have in the United States. People cannot speak to each other. Trump can't get the best lawyers in the country to represent him, because people have told me we don't want to be "Dershowitzed." We don't want to have happened to us and our family what happened to you. My wife for example, was working out in a gym. A woman walked in and said, "I can't be in the same room with Alan Dershowitz's wife." I was seated next to Caroline Kennedy at a dinner party. And she said, "If I knew you had been invited, I wouldn't have come." Suggesting that she couldn't be in the same room with me.

This is the woman who's the ambassador to Australia, has to negotiate with foreign leaders. She can't be in the same room with somebody because he defended Donald Trump under the Constitution. That's the climate that I write about in my book, *The Price of Principle*. I have tried very hard to stick to the same principles I've had for nearly sixty years fighting McCarthyism, fighting denial of due process, fighting for free speech for everybody, not for me, but also for thee. And for that, I've paid a heavy price. My wife has paid a heavy price. My children have paid a heavy price, but most important, the people who want to hear me at the library in Chilmark and other places that I've been canceled, have no ability to hear me. That violates their First Amendment rights as well as mine.

Gerry Baker: I guess, to play devil's advocate a little bit here. President Biden's been talking about MAGA the faction, obviously Donald Trump by extension, as semi-fascist. And I suppose this is why people feel so strong. I mean, you can disagree with that. I don't even know what it means, semi-fascist, but there are people who think, quite serious people, and you encounter them all the time who think that Trump represents a kind of unique fascistic threat to democracy, and that this calls for something way beyond the kind of the normal politics of constitutional and democratic procedures. He's a unique missile aimed at our democratic institution.

Alan Dershowitz: I agree with you completely. And let's remember too, that there's a totalitarian mindset among some Trump supporters, but there is a totalitarian mindset among woke people on the hard left. Some of the leading academics today are calling for the end of the Constitution, the end of free speech, the end of due process saying these are patriarchal supremacist notions written into a Constitution that was drafted by slave owners. So, we're seeing totalitarian instincts on both ends of the spectrum. And I've always said that the hard, hard right is closer to the hard, hard left than either of them are to the true conservatives and true liberals. I think of myself as a true libertarian liberal who opposes any kind of totalitarian mindset. And I don't like to use the word fascist. I don't think the president should use that word because it connotes Nazi Germany and fascist Italy. And we're not anywhere close to any of that, but we're in trouble. We're in deep trouble, because the hard left and the hard right have both shown intolerance. And for good reason. If you think you have the truth with a capital T, why do you need free speech? Why do you need dissent? Why do you need due process? We know who's guilty and who's innocent. Why do you need trials? That's the end of democracy. And it's coming as much from the left as from the right. And it's more dangerous from the left. Let me tell you why. The right is largely the past. The left is the future. The hard left people are teaching and propagandizing our college students today. People who ten years from now will be the heads of corporations, the heads of media, people will be in Congress. They'll be running for president of the United States in twenty years. And today they're being propagandized by professors and by fellow students who do not believe in free speech and due process and believe that the ends justify the means. That's why the hard left today is actually more dangerous than the hard right. And I wish

President Biden would spend some time attacking people who vote for him on the hard left, because that's the obligation of every decent person. You attack the people who are closest to you. As a liberal, as a person who has been identified with the left, I spend much more time attacking the left than I do attacking the right. And I think President Biden should do the same thing.

Gerry Baker: Alan Dershowitz, I'm sure a lot of people are listening to this will agree with you. Alan Dershowitz, thanks very much indeed for joining us.

Alan Dershowitz: My pleasure. Thank you

"Get Trump!" Damn the Constitution

A scene from the film *A Man for All Seasons* well illustrates the current debate about the compromising the Constitution to get Trump:

> **William Roper:** "So, now you give the Devil the benefit of law!"
> **Sir Thomas More:** "Yes! What would you do? Cut a great road through the law to get after the Devil?"
> **William Roper:** "Yes, I'd cut down every law in England to do that!"
> **Sir Thomas More:** "Oh? And when the last law was down, and the Devil turned 'round on you, where would you hide, Roper, the laws all being flat? This country is planted thick with laws, from coast to coast, Man's laws, not God's! And if you cut them down, and you're just the man to do it, do you really think you could stand upright

in the winds that would blow then? Yes, I'd give the Devil
benefit of law, for my own safety's sake!"

Today on the left, there are more Ropers than Mores. Sam
Harris, for example, has proclaimed that he is willing to break
democracy to save democracy. Others, too, have expressed a
willingness to cut down the Constitution to get the devil.
Today's devil is Trump, and today's Ropers are willing to "cut
a great road through the law to get after [today's] devil." Like
More, I would give everyone "the benefit of law," but not
only "for my own safety's sake," but for the sake of future
generations. Once the Constitution and civil liberties are
"cut down," it is difficult to regrow them and the "winds that
would blow them" might prevent us from "standing upright"
against new tyrannies from the extreme left and right.

There is a legitimate way to stop Trump from being elected
in 2024, just as he was not elected in 2020: a fair election
defeated him once, and it can do so again—without cutting
down the Constitution and weakening the rule of law. But it
will take hard work, not unconstitutional shortcuts.

The Pros and Cons of a Special Prosecutor for Trump

Attorney General Merrick Garland has appointed Jack
Smith as a special prosecutor to investigate Donald Trump.
The decision was made after Trump announced his candidacy for president. The purpose of a special prosecutor is to
avoid both the reality and perception of political bias that
is inherent in an attorney general investigating his boss's
potential political opponent.

The positive side of a special prosecutor is that he is independent of the attorney general and other high-ranking Justice Department officials who were appointed by the incumbent president and can be fired or promoted by him. This is not to suggest that any of these people would be overtly influenced by a political consideration rather than by the rule of law. Such bias is, of course possible, either at a conscious or unconscious level, but even if it did not exist in reality, the widespread perception would be that it was there. Justice must not only be done, but it must also be seen to be done. This is especially important in our current age of highly divisive partisan politics.

By all accounts, Jack Smith fits the bill for independence and professionalism. He has a long career as a state, federal, and international prosecutor. His experience makes it highly likely that he will conduct an objective investigation. But whichever way it turns out, Smith will be attacked: partisan Republicans will criticize him if he finds against Trump, while partisan Democrats will object if he finds in his favor. It is a no-win situation for anyone interested in popularity or a political future. Previous special prosecutors, such as the late Ken Starr, understood this when they took the job, but they placed patriotism over careerism.

The role of a special prosecutors is unlike that of a general prosecutor because special prosecutors have a specific target. Prosecutorial discretion is a central, perhaps the central, aspect of the job of ordinary prosecutors. They not only decide if the criminal law was technically violated, they also look at every case against the background of similar cases that either were or were not prosecuted. This is especially important in a high visibility and divisive case like that of Donald Trump.

Assume for example that an investigation concludes that he was technically guilty of violating statutes regarding the mishandling of classified or secret documents. But also assume that the investigation concludes that his misbehavior was not significantly worse than Hillary Clinton's, who was also a presidential candidate. An ordinary prosecutor can undertake a comparative analysis such as the one undertaken by the prosecutors and the FBI in the Hillary Clinton case. They concluded that no one had previously been prosecuted for comparable conduct. A special prosecutor is less likely to make a comparative judgment, although his mandate would not preclude that.

The job of an ordinary prosecutor is to investigate crimes in general and prioritize those that should be prosecuted. They do not ordinarily focus on the individual first and then seek to determine whether he has committed any crimes. But that is precisely what special prosecutors do. As the old expression goes, "to a hammer, everything is a nail." To a special prosecutor, his target may well be presumed guilty, rather than innocent. This is not inevitable, but it is more likely with regard to a special prosecutor rather than an ordinary one.

No one should rush to judgment about Garland's decision to appoint a special prosecutor. Garland is a decent man, a highly respected former judge, and someone who has not immersed himself in partisan politics. His choice of special prosecutor also seems suitable to the job. But it remains to be seen whether Smith and his staff will be able to resist the enormous partisan pressures that will be placed on them.

Thus far, the investigations of Trump and his associates have not passed the test either of justice being done or being seen to be done. An aura of partisanship has permeated most of the investigations, especially those conducted by the House January 6 Committee and by New York Attorney General Letitia James, who campaigned on the promise to get Trump. How several of Trump's associates have been arrested and handcuffed has also lent credibility to claims of partisanship as did the use of a broad warrant instead of a narrower subpoena in the search of Mar-a-Lago.

Accordingly, a special prosecutor must be "Caesar's wife" when it comes to conducting investigations of a Republican candidate for president. Anything short of complete objectivity and compliance with the rule of law will only exacerbate the partisan divisions that currently plague our country.

Biden's Classification Mess Will Help Trump

The recent disclosure that President Biden had stored classified material that he obtained while vice president in a private facility will make it more difficult for Attorney General Eric Garland to prosecute Donald Trump for his mishandling of classified information.

There may well be considerable differences between the Biden and Trump cases, but the headline is the same: Biden and Trump both mishandled classified information. That is the way the public will perceive the two cases, regardless of what the special prosecutors and investigators may find. If Attorney General Garland treats the two cases significantly differently—if he allows the prosecution of Trump without allowing prosecution of Biden—many in the public will perceive a double standard. This is especially problematic since our nation is so bitterly divided and it is likely that the 2024 election will pit Trump against Biden. Any prosecutorial decision regarding these two candidates will surely become a divisive political issue in the 2024 campaigns.

Even before the recent Biden disclosures, I argued that in order for the Justice Department to prosecute Donald Trump for what was found at Mar-a-Lago, two standards would have to be met. The first is the Richard Nixon standard: Nixon was removed from office not as a result of pressure from Democrats, but rather by threats from Republican leaders that he would be impeached and prosecuted if he did not resign. This bipartisan support gave credibility to his removal.

The second standard is what I call the Hillary Clinton and Sandy Berger comparisons. In order to prosecute Trump for his mishandling of classified material, the evidence would have to show considerable differences between what Trump is accused of doing and what the two Democrats were accused of doing. Now that standard has been expanded to include the Clinton-Berger-Biden episodes. The evidence must show dispositive differences between the three Democrats who were not prosecuted and Donald Trump.

On the basis of currently available evidence, neither of these standards has been met. Perhaps new evidence will be disclosed that warrant prosecution of Trump without any suspicion of partisan double standard. Attorney General Garland understands that his job is to make sure not only that justice is done, but that it is seen to be done. The recent Biden disclosures would likely make that impossible, especially in the current bipartisan environment.

Then there is the issue of timing. Why did the Biden administration delay disclosure of the Biden issue until now. According to media reports, the disclosure came only after it was clear that it would be reported in the press. If true, that raises the question of whether it would have been reported at all, had the media not gotten wind of it. It also raises the question of who disclosed this information to the media.

Many Republicans claim that failure to disclose Biden's mishandling of classified material before the midterm elections may have been intended to prevent it's having an impact on the election. We know that timing can be everything when it comes to voting. The decision by former FBI director James Comey to disclose the reopening of the investigation against Hillary Clinton on the eve of the 2016 election, may well have impacted her narrow loss. We will never know.

It may be understandable that disclosure was not made in the week between its discovery and the election, but it is hard to explain the additional two-month delay. Although the Biden episode may be entirely innocent, as I believe it probably was, the public had the right to make that judgment in real time. They also have the right to know that Biden quickly turned over the material to the archives and that his lawyers have apparently cooperated fully with investigations. This contrasts sharply with what Trump and his legal team did and did not do.

The law and practice regarding presidential and vice-presidential material is anything but clear. This is especially true when it comes to the possibility of criminal prosecution. It is highly unlikely now that anyone—Republican or Democrat—will be prosecuted for the mishandling of classified information after they leave office. The law should be clarified, and the criminal law should be made applicable only to willful mishandling of highly sensitive material that endangers national security.

Garland Appoints a Special Prosecutor for Biden

It is often said that justice must not only be <u>done</u>, but must be <u>seen</u>. The appointment for the special prosecutor to investigate President Biden's alleged mishandling of classified information was made not for justice to be done, but rather for the appearance of justice to be satisfied.

Everyone knows that President Biden will not be indicted for classified material showing up in various locations. First of all, a sitting president cannot constitutionally be indicted. The Justice Department recognizes that in its own rules and guidelines. Nor is this a case where others may be subject to indictment. Finally, even if Biden were to be found to have committed criminal offenses, they would not rise to the level of high crimes and misdemeanors, which are the criteria for impeachment.

So why then did Attorney General Garland appoint a special prosecutor? The answer is clear: because he had previously appointed a special prosecutor to investigate Donald Trump. Since both men are likely to be running against each other for president, it is imperative that they be treated equally. Even if the facts differ somewhat, the bottom line is both seem to have mishandled classified material.

At a time when Americans are deeply divided and agree about so little, there is one conclusion that seems to unite us all: The vast majority of Americans strongly believe that there are differences between what Biden and Trump allegedly did. That's the agreement. But this agreement is that half the country seems to believe that what Biden did was worse, while the other half believe that what Trump did was worse. Very few seem to believe that they are equally culpable.

My own belief is that every president and vice president has probably mishandled classified material in some way. This is not because of any malevolent intent. None has given or sold such material to our enemies. The mishandling was probably either careless or designed to help a former official in writing their memoirs. The case of Sandy Berger is an example of the latter. He stuffed improperly possessed material into his socks to facilitate writing his memoir. The other recent examples—Hillary Clinton, Donald Trump, and Joe Biden—seem like instances of sloppiness, laziness, or convenience.

There should be full investigations of all of these breaches of security, so that Congress can clarify and tighten up the rules. It should not be the law that the president can declassify anything, without notifying anybody or making any record. But that seems to be the current rule, at least as it applies to potential criminal liability. But special prosecutors are not supposed to be appointed to do general investigations leading to changes in the law. That is the job of Congress. Special prosecutors are supposed to determine whether their target should be indicted and prosecuted. We can be fairly certain that the end result of these investigations will be decisions not to prosecute either Biden or Trump.

Even if one or both special prosecutors were to recommend indictment—an unlikely prospect—Attorney General

Garland would not follow their advice. He understands that if only one of them were to be prosecuted, the divisions in this country would be greatly exacerbated. So the end result will be that neither is prosecuted.

In our current world of tit for tat, these alleged violations cancel each other out. This may not be the case as a matter of law—one may be far more criminal than the other—but it is certainly so as a matter of realpolitik. And we live in a world where the law bends to politics.

So let both special prosecutors spin their wheels. Let them dig deeply. Perhaps they will find new evidence that distinguishes the case so sharply that the public would accept the prosecution of one without the other. But this is highly unlikely. Each side will continue to claim that the other is more at fault and should be prosecuted. These partisan demands for "justice for me but not for thee" will also cancel each other out in the court of public opinion.

The Democrats started all this by their showy overreaction to Trump's derelictions, manifested by an unjustified search and seizure. President Biden couldn't understand how a president could be so insensitive to security concerns by putting sources and methods at risk. Now former president Trump is throwing that statement back at his rival. That is what the tit for tat weaponization of justice has done. We are all the poorer for it.

Why Charging Alec Baldwin with Manslaughter Is Wrong

The willingness of prosecutors and politicians to attach the criminal law to fit targets is not limited to political enemies. The Alec Baldwin prosecution illustrates how vague, open-ended laws can be stretched to fit celebrities in high-profile cases.

Prosecutors in New Mexico are wrong in charging the actor Alec Baldwin with manslaughter in the accidental shooting of Halyna Hutchins. It is clear Baldwin did not intend to fire a loaded gun. It was a tragic accident, and accidents are not generally crimes, unless they involve some criminal state of mind. Whenever an innocent person is killed by the actions of another and there is a temptation to look for criminal liability on the part of the shooter, sometimes it can be found. Other times it cannot.

In this case, Baldwin claims that he was explicitly told the gun did not contain live ammunition. Even if prosecutors can cast doubt on this self-serving statement, it will be impossible for them to prove beyond a reasonable doubt that Baldwin believed he was risking Hutchins's life by pulling the trigger or cocking the gun.

As Baldwin previously said in an interview "someone is responsible for what happened, and I can't say who that is, but I know it's not me." It is true that someone, or several people, were responsible for allowing live ammunition to be in a gun that would be fired on the set. But absent a conspiracy—and there is no evidence that one existed here—criminal guilt is personal. Prosecutors would have to prove not that there was negligence on the set, but that Baldwin himself was personally responsible for the gross negligence that led to Halyna Hutchins's death. Based on the evidence that has been made public, that burden will not be able to be met. An actor, even one who was also a producer, is entitled to rely on the assurance of the person responsible for armaments that he had been given a gun with no live ammunition.

New Mexico's statute defining involuntary manslaughter, like the laws in many other states, vests enormous discretion in prosecutors because the terms of the statute are vague and subject to multiple interpretations. Here is what Section 30-2-3B provides: "Involuntary manslaughter consists of manslaughter committed in the commission of an unlawful act not amounting to felony, or in the commission of a lawful act which might produce death in an unlawful manner or without due caution and circumspection."

What constitutes "due caution and circumspection" is unclear as is the concept of a lawful act that might produce death "in an unlawful manner."

Thomas Jefferson once said that for a criminal statute to be constitutional it must be capable of being understood by a person who reads it "while running." Quite an interesting image! I am reading the statute while sitting, after studying and teaching criminal and constitutional law for more than half a century, and I'm not sure what it means. It is hard to imagine that Alec Baldwin could read this statute and understand that firing a gun that he had been told contained no live ammunition would either be an unlawful act or a lawful act that might produce deaths in an unlawful manner.

Early in our history the courts held that crimes must be narrowly defined and reasonably understandable from reading preexisting statutes. Criminal law, unlike tort and contract law, is governed by statutes, not by common law. Vague terms cannot be fitted onto tragic circumstances that call out for retribution.

New Mexico prosecutors may receive some solace from a highly publicized accidental shooting case in Minnesota that resulted in the conviction and imprisonment of a police officer. Former officer Kim Potter believed she was firing a taser at a fleeing felon. But she had accidentally pulled her wrong firearm and shot the victim with live ammunition, killing him. There was no dispute that Potter shot the wrong gun by accident. So despite her long record of distinguished service to the police, she was convicted. That case is now on appeal and the conviction should be reversed, but because of the current atmosphere surrounding police shootings of African American men (the victim in the Potter case was a teenager), it is possible that the Minnesota appellate courts will come to the wrong decision.

But two wrongs do not make a right. The criminal law should be reserved for willful, deliberate, and intentional actions. At the very least, if negligence can serve as a basis for conviction, it should be the kind of negligence that the defendant could have anticipated would produce a tragic outcome.

Alec Baldwin is a rich and powerful celebrity. The law must be applied fairly to him, as it would be to others. Sometimes people like Baldwin are advantaged by their celebrity. Sometimes they are disadvantaged. The question is whether this criminal prosecution would have been brought if the person firing the gun was unknown. In a previous case, an actor named Brandon Lee was accidentally shot and killed by a gun loaded with blanks, which unbeknownst to the shooter had shards of metal in the barrel that caused the tragic death. The shooter in that case was not charged, but the participants were sued civilly. (I consulted on that case.) That seems like the right decision. Everyone involved in the Baldwin case has been sued, and some have settled. That too seems like the right resolution to a tragic accident.

X

The Complicity of Media and Academia

Our constitutional system of separation of powers and checks and balances includes only government institutions: the executive, legislative, and judicial branches. But non-governmental institutions—such as the media, academia, and religion—also play an important role in checking governmental abuses. The First Amendment—separating church from state, and precluding governmental control over the press—provides additional checks against tyranny. In this chapter, I focus on the failure of these extra governmental branches, which are protected by the First Amendment, to provide neutral checks. In other words, instead of being a part of the solution to partisan excesses, many of them have become part of the problem. They, too, are seeking to get Trump—to prevent him from regaining the presidency—by employing unprincipled and dangerous means.

Did Twitter Suppress Hunter Biden Laptop Story Ahead of the 2020 Presidential Election

The promised disclosure by Elon Musk of the real story behind Twitter's refusal to tweet the *New York Post* reporting on Hunter Biden's laptop fell short of a "bombshell." But it contained troubling information about the possible role of government actors in this pre-election decision.

The reporter to whom Musk provided his disclosure talked about the influence of "connected actors." Neither the names nor statuses of these actors were provided—at least not yet. But the context suggests that the heavy thumb of government actors may have weighed—either directly or indirectly—on the censorial decisions of Twitter. The First Amendment does not prohibit Twitter, a private company, from censoring on partisan or any other grounds. It does prohibit the government from censoring, except in extraordinary circumstances not relevant to the Hunter Biden laptop.

So, the questions are: Did government actors play any role in Twitter's decisions? If so, how much of a role? Was governmental pressure, direct or indirect, employed? If so, by whom? And how much? Are government actors continuing to influence decisions by other social media? Do government agents have compelling, nonpartisan, reasons for intruding? Or was the intrusion designed to help Democrats in the imminent election?

If Musk knows the answers to any or all of these important questions, I hope he provides them in subsequent disclosures because they are important. The public has the right to know what role government actors may have played in censoring information that may have influenced—rightly or wrongly—some voters.

Social media, especially Twitter, have the capacity to influence the outcome of elections. Donald Trump understood and made use of this relatively new tool during his campaigns and his presidency. There is a debate raging as to whether the government has any power under the First Amendment to regulate these powerful tools. There is no reasonable debate over whether government actors should have the power to manipulate these tools for partisan advantage. They should not, especially if they exercise that power surreptitiously and without transparency.

That is the real danger to democracy, the rule of law and the marketplace of ideas: government actors secretly manipulating private media to achieve partisan goals by censoring outside the protection of the First Amendment. If that is what occurred in the incident involving Twitter censorship of the *New York Post*'s reporting about the Hunter Biden laptop on the eve a national election, then it clearly implicates the First Amendment. The government may not do secretly what it could not do openly. Nor can it use a private company to circumvent its constitutional obligation not to censor.

So, let's get all the facts surrounding Twitter's decision to censor the *New York Post*'s reporting on the Hunter Biden laptop. Let's learn who these "connected actors" are. And if they are government officials who applied pressure on Twitter to censor a story that might have changed the outcome of any elections or influenced public opinion against other public officials, then they must be held accountable.

Twitter's Ban on Kanye West Violates Its Own Policies

Twitter's decision to ban Kanye West raises interesting issues about freedom of speech. Since both Twitter and West are private citizens, the First Amendment is not directly implicated, but its spirit cannot be ignored.

Let's begin with an indisputable fact: Ye (the former Kanye West) is a virulent anti-Semite who has called for "death con 3" against the Jewish people. He has made other anti-Semitic statements as well.

The image that got him banned juxtaposes the Star of David, a symbol of Judaism for millennia, with the Nazi swastika, the symbol of Hitler's murder of 6 million Jews. West claims that this juxtaposition is a sign of love. No, it is a sign of hate.

But hate speech is protected under the First Amendment. It also seems to be permitted by Elon Musk's new anti-censorship policies at Twitter. These policies do not allow censorship on the basis of offensiveness or disagreement, but they do ban users from inciting violence.

So, the question is whether or not West is inciting violence in violation of Twitter standards. I do not believe he is. Incitement has a specific meaning. It generally requires oral communication urging imminent violence. It rarely covers the written word, and I know of no case where it covers symbols such as the swastika imposed on the Jewish star.

So, if Twitter had been the government, it would be unconstitutional to prohibit the swastika and Jewish star symbol, despicable and hateful as that is. But because Twitter is not the government it has considerable leeway in deciding who shall have access to its platform. It also has leeway in what constitutes incitement, but I think Musk is wrong in categorizing the obnoxious juxtaposition as incitement.

Beyond the specific facts of this troubling action and reaction, Musk's decision brings to the surface a simmering dispute about the role of giant social media companies—such as Twitter, Facebook, and YouTube—in regulating communications which are offensive and sometimes dangerous.

There are those who claim that these media giants should be viewed as quasi-governmental, and thus subject to some restrictions on their ability to censor. They analogize them to "common carriers," such as trains and buses, which even though privately owned, are subject to state regulation. But these common carriers are not involved in the dissemination of speech.

A closer analogy would be the telegraph and telephone companies. But these, too, are different from modern media. The telephone and telegraph involve private communications between individuals. Social media involves public communications that are accessed by millions of viewers and readers.

Any attempt by the government to regulate social media would directly involve the First Amendment. These private companies have their own First Amendment rights to decide what to publish and what to censor. When the *Miami Herald* refused to publish a letter to the editor by a public figure who had been unfairly criticized, the Supreme Court held that the First Amendment precluded the government from requiring a newspaper to publish a letter to the editor. Again, newspapers, which were widely available when our Bill of Rights was ratified, are significantly different from current social media.

The current social media entities do, however, benefit from government action. Congress enacted a law protecting social media from various legal liabilities to which newspapers are subject. This makes sense, because items posted on social media are automatic and immediate. The social media companies, generally, lack the ability to prevent the real-time posting, though they can take them down once they become aware of their content. Newspapers on the other hand publish nothing unless the editor approves in advance.

The fact that social media have been given special privileges by legislation makes them different from newspapers and even conventional television stations. But these privileges would seem insufficient to empower the government to impose censorship.

The issues raised by Twitter's decision to ban Kanye West are some of the most complex and difficult ones regarding free speech. There is no perfect answer to the question of whether giant social media companies that today control so much communication should be subject to any government regulation.

For originalists, it is impossible to know with certainty what Jefferson and Madison would have said about the claim by media companies that they are entitled to censor speech on the basis of their First Amendment rights. Nor can advocates of a living constitution provide a single correct answer to this question. It is a work in progress that may ultimately be influenced by how these media companies employ their power to decide what will be communicated and what will be banned.

Elon Musk has promised a more permissive approach for Twitter than those taken by Facebook and YouTube. Yet he, too, has felt the need to censor hate speech, claiming it constituted incitement. Although I find West's juxtaposition of the Star of David and the swastika beneath contempt, I do not believe it should have been censored by Twitter as incitement.

Berkeley Clubs Ban Zionist Speakers

Fourteen clubs officially sponsored by the University of California at Berkeley School of Law have "Zionist-free zones" that some say are reminiscent of the early twentieth-century signs that reportedly said, "No Jews or dogs allowed." Are these clubs merely exercising their First Amendment rights by banning all Zionist speakers and *only* Zionist speakers? This is the question that is roiling not only the UC Berkeley campus, but campuses all across the country that see the answer setting a precedent for them.

Let us begin with the undisputed facts.

Fourteen clubs have amended their charters to disallow all Zionist speakers—even if they also support Palestinian rights and other progressive causes—and even if they intend to speak on a subject unrelated to Israel. If they are Zionists, they are not welcome to speak at these clubs about anything!

The alleged justification for this total ban on all Zionists—that is, people who believe that Israel has a right to exist—is to protect the *safety* and welfare of Palestinian students. This is patent nonsense. No students have been physically threatened by Zionists, and no student is entitled to be protected from ideas.

These clubs include the Berkeley Law Muslim Student Association, Middle Eastern and North African Law Students Association, Women of Color Collective, Asian

Pacific American Law Students Association, Queer Caucus, Community Defense Project, Women of Berkeley Law, and Law Students of African Descent.

In other words, even Muslims, gays, feminists, and supporters of progressive causes seem to be excluded if they also believe Israel has the right to exist. By excluding ALL Zionists, the ban seems to cover Jews who favor a two-state solution, a return to the 1967 lines, and a right of return for all Palestinians.

Those clubs are engaging in a combination of Stalinism and anti-Semitism: Stalinism in the sense that they allow no dissenting views from their "politically correct" doctrine of no Israel; anti-Semitism in the sense that among all the nations of the world which are involved in controversies—Russia, Iran, China, Belarus, to name a few—they have singled out for banning only the nation-state of the Jewish people.

Imagine if a university club were to exclude all speakers who support Black Lives Matter? The current ban is even worse because it seems to ban all Zionist speakers—regardless of their views—from organizations that have nothing to do with Israel. A Jewish feminist could not speak to the women of UC Berkeley about abortion if it were discovered that she is a Zionist. That is pure bigotry.

The University of California at Berkeley is a public institution. If it in any way supports these organizations—financially or by allowing them to have offices on the campus—then it is effectively the State of California that is enacting and enforcing these bans. This constitutes state action and is governed by the First Amendment. The question is which way the First Amendment cuts. Does it give the

clubs the right to exclude all speakers who are Zionists? Or
does it prohibit state actors from demanding that all speakers disavow Zionism as a condition to exercising their First
Amendment right to speak? And what about the rights of
their potential audience members to hear them? The answers
may also implicate federal funding for the university.

Clubs and universities generally have a right to choose
their speakers, but there is a vast difference between indi-
vidually deciding who will speak and making a collective
decision banning all people of a particular ideology, religion,
or race. This is particularly so when the ideology serves as
a mask for anti-Semitism. Not all Jews are Zionists. Not
all support Israel. Many, including me, disagree with some
of Israel's policies, just as I disagree with some policies of
every country, including the United States. Not all African
Americans support Black Lives Matter, but enough do so
that such a ban would constitute racial discrimination, just
as a ban on all Zionists constitutes anti-Semitism.

These clubs are effectively banning most Jews. The dean
of UC Berkeley School of Law implicitly made this point
when he said that 90 percent of Berkeley's Jews, including
him, would be banned by such a policy. This is discrimination pure and simple. The dean also said that he would discipline any club that actually discriminated on religious or
"viewpoint" grounds. I hereby volunteer to present the case
for Israel—or for gay marriage—at any or all of these clubs.
It will be interesting to see if they exclude me—a proud, if
sometimes critical, Jewish Zionist.

Although the current ban is only for speakers, its "logic"—
protecting the safety of Palestinian students—would extend
to membership, even presence, at these clubs.

The dean also said that school policy prohibits discrimination in membership based on religion or point of view. This would seem to conflict with the "safety" rationale for the ban.

The ban is, sadly, also akin to a "loyalty oath" of the kind imposed by McCarthyites in the 1950s and opposed back then by both liberals and civil libertarians. Today's liberals and civil libertarians should also strongly oppose these ideological tests as well. But because they come from the intersectionalist left, many are silent, while others are complicit.

Kudos to the dean for condemning this bigotry, even while he defends their constitutional right to practice it. I have offered to publicly debate or discuss our different views of how the First Amendment impacts this ban.

Universities have an educational and moral duty to foster dialogue and learning, not banning and censorship. Public universities have a constitutional obligation to prohibit religious and ethnic discrimination. Berkeley is failing both tests.

The question remains: Is their failure protected or prohibited by the First Amendment?

Is the Jewish Democratic Council Really Jewish—or Just Democrats?

As President Joe Biden was returning from his productive trip to the Middle East, the Jewish Democratic Council was holding a fundraiser on Martha's Vineyard to support Democratic candidates in the 2022 midterm elections and to help elect a Democratic president in 2024. Former president Bill Clinton and former senator Hillary Clinton were the guests of honor and speakers, thus suggesting that this organization purports to represent mainstream Jewish Democrats.

But it does not. It represents the left wing of the Democratic Party. It certainly does not represent mainstream Jewish voters who care about Israel and the growing threat of anti-Semitism.

At this so-called "Jewish" event, there was no discussion of Israel, or the existential threat it faces as Iran comes closer to constructing a nuclear arsenal. Nor was there any discussion of the increasing anti-Semitism within the so-called "progressive" wing of the Democratic Party, or of the decreasing support for Israel among some younger Democrats and among some Democratic office holders. Not a single word about issues of deep concern to most American Jews!

New York Times columnist Tom Friedman recently predicted that Biden might be the last pro-Israel Democratic presidential candidate. Among those being considered to replace Biden either in 2024 or 2028 are several who are stridently anti-Israel and some who are lukewarm. Current Democratic Members of the House include some who wrongly regard Israel as an apartheid state akin to South Africa until 1993, and others who would cut off military assistance to the nation state of the Jewish people. Still others, including some Democratic senators, are hyper-critical of Israel and want to see a reassessment of United States policy toward our strongest ally in the Middle East.

Had I attended the Martha's Vineyard event, I would have expressed my concerns about the growing abandonment of Israel by the left wing of the Democratic Party. But they obviously do not want to hear the perspective of this Jewish Democrat, because the organization is more united behind social policy issues—abortion, gun control, the environment, and the Supreme Court—than they are about Israel. I was told by two people who attended the event that the word "Israel" was never even mentioned, although Biden's recent visit to Israel was headline news. The omission of Israel was confirmed by the organization's own website.

It is difficult to imagine any other ethnic or other group of Democrats—Blacks, Arabs, gays—that would not even mention the issues of direct concern to that group at a large fundraiser. Why are Jewish Democrats different?

This organization—the Jewish Democratic Council—is misnamed. It recruits members and solicits money based on false advertising. It promotes itself as comprised of pro-Israel Jews. But the reality is that its leadership consists mainly of progressive Democrats who just happen to be Jewish. For them, Israel, Iran, and anti-Semitism are peripheral issues. That is increasingly true of many Democratic Jewish voters who prioritize other concerns over Israel, over the growing threat of anti-Semitism from the hard left and hard right, and over other issues that directly affect the Jewish people.

I shake my head in frustration at why so many left-wing Jewish Democrats are willing to abandon Israel and continue to vote blindly for their grandparents' Democratic Party without demanding that it marginalize its anti-Israel extremists. I understand the reluctance of some traditional Jewish Democrats to vote for Republicans who oppose liberal social policies. I share that reluctance. Hence my frustration.

More and more Jews are expressing this frustration by voting for candidates who support Israel without regard to their party identification. To paraphrase former president Ronald Reagan: they do not believe they have left the Democratic

Party; they believe the Democratic Party is leaving the millions of Jews who think more like moderate Republicans such as Mitt Romney than radical Democrats such as Bernie Sanders.

Many, like me, will continue to vote for and contribute to the candidates who we think are best (or least worse) for our country, for the world, and for Israel. We expect that these candidates will generally be Democrats. But if they are not, then we will vote for their opponent. We have no loyalty to the current Democrat Party, just as many of its most prominent officials seem to have no loyalty to so many of their Jewish supporters. We certainly should have no loyalty to organizations such as the Jewish Democratic Council that hides its true priorities behind the misleading label "Jewish." There is nothing Jewish about their agenda, which is to elect Democrats regardless of their views on issues of direct concern to the Jewish community and Israel.

Is Dobbs the First Case to Take Rights Away from Americans?

Whatever one may think of *Dobbs v. Mississippi*, the Supreme Court decision overruling *Roe v. Wade*, some critics have overstated its uniqueness in taking from Americans their preexisting rights. Professor Laurence Tribe badly misinformed his readers when he said the following:

> Friday was a singular day in our history: the first day in living memory that Americans went to bed with fewer inalienable rights than they had when they woke up. Not just in living memory. Ever.

Tragically, there have been dozens of cases throughout our history in which Americans had their most fundamental rights taken away. Tribe's historical memory is blinded by his partisanship. Let's look at the real history.

The Alien and Sedition laws took away the right to criticize elected officials, which was granted just a few years earlier by the First Amendment. The Dred Scott case denied Black Americans the right of citizenship, and even personhood. Several cases, during that same period, denied Native Americans their fundamental rights. *Buck v. Bell* authorized the sterilization of allegedly unfit citizens, thus taking away their reproductive rights. In *Korematsu v. US*, more than 100,000 American citizens of Japanese ethnicity were denied the right to be free. In several cases during the McCarthy period, Americans were denied the right to belong to the Communist Party. In *Bowers v. Hardwick*, gay and lesbian Americans were denied the right to sexual freedom. Capital defendants were denied the right to life when the Supreme Court essentially reversed its decision outlawing capital punishment. At the beginning of the twentieth century, many Americans were denied the right to be united with their families when racist immigration laws were enacted, limiting the number of ethnic minorities that were permitted to become citizens.

In addition to those rights, most of which today are recognized, many Americans over the years were denied rights which some, but not others, deemed fundamental, such as the right to pray in schools, the right of Mormons to practice polygamy, property rights under the early New Deal, and the right to travel freely and not wear masks during the COVID-19 pandemic. The Violent Crime Control and

Law Enforcement Act of 1994 severely limited the rights of defendants to habeas corpus. And now, many Americans, including Tribe himself, would severely curtail what many Americans believe is their Second Amendment right to "keep and bear Arms."

Tribe's blanket statement that never in history have Americans gone to bed with fewer rights than when they woke up is not only ignorant historically and constitutionally, but also extremely insensitive to African Americans, Native Americans, the mentally ill, Japanese Americans, and other marginalized groups that have been denied the most basic rights over the years.

The truth, which Tribe denies in the interest of his partisan narrative, is that the pendulum of rights has swung widely throughout our history. Even if Martin Luther King Jr. was correct when he said, "The arc of the moral universe is long, but it bends towards justice," that arc has not always pointed in the direction of rights—or justice. In a democracy with a complex system of separation of powers, checks and balances, and federalism, there will always be some back and forth with regard to rights. As Roger Baldwin, the founder of the American Civil Liberties Union, put it: "The struggle for liberty never stays won." So, too, with the eternal struggle for rights. Tribe seems to take for granted that his preferred rights are an ever-expanding given.

He is wrong. We must not assume that rights, once recognized, will never be taken away. We must persist in struggling to preserve them, through the courts, legislatures, executives, constitutional amendments, public opinion, and other lawful means.

No one benefits from false and ideologically driven history of the kind that Tribe and his ilk try to sell in reaction to this wrongful decision. Falsehoods will not set us free. Only hard work, based on truth, will push the arc toward justice.

Garland Memo on Parent Protests May Chill Free Speech

Attorney General Merrick Garland recently released a memorandum addressing "a disturbing spike in harassment, intimidation, and threats of violence against school administrators, board members, teachers, and staff. . . ." The actual words of the memorandum—the lyrics—seem appropriate on their face, but the music is discordant with the First Amendment.

The memo acknowledges that "spirited debate about policy matters is protected under our Constitution." It then goes on to direct the FBI to come up with strategies for addressing illegal threats against these public officials. Nothing wrong with that. But no similar memo was directed against Black Lives Matter and other far-left groups that not only threaten violence against public officials and private citizens, but also engage in a considerable amount of criminal conduct, such as arson and destruction of property. Some protesters have intimidated and threatened people who disagree with them. Although no specific mention was made of parents' protests against teaching critical race theory and comparable ideological content to school children, or against mandatory masking requirements, it is clear from the context and timing that these are the protests that generated this memo.

As a result of this timing, context, and apparent lack of concern for the Black Lives Matter type of protests, many parents are understandably worried that the Justice

Department may be engaged in selective investigations and ultimately selective prosecutions. Again, the absence of certain notes makes the concerns expressed by protesting parents understandable.

When dealing with protests, the Justice Department must be clear that the First Amendment fully protects all forms of protest, including raucous and unpleasant ones, and that generalized threats and nonviolent intimidation do not overcome this constitutional protection. Protesters must specifically threaten immediate violence against specific individuals. The Supreme Court has upheld vague, generalized advocacy of violence as protected by the First Amendment.

The Garland memo fails to draw the appropriate First Amendment line and suggests that the FBI and other law enforcement agencies can appropriately investigate and "discourage" generalized threats and "efforts to intimidate" public officials. While the First Amendment errs on the side of protecting such wrongheaded protests, the Garland memo errs on the side of investigating and possibly prosecuting them.

The most distressing aspect of this memorandum is its apparent focus on right-wing activities, as distinguished from equally dangerous left-wing activities. The rule of law must always pass the "shoe on the other foot test." It must make it clear that the Justice Department does not distinguish between what it regards as "good" protest activities and "bad" ones based on political preferences.

Back in the day, the American Civil Liberties Union could be counted on to express concern that memos of this kind might "discourage" or deter more than illegal activities, but may also chill constitutionally protected ones, since no one wants to be investigated by the FBI. In the past, the ACLU vigorously protected the rights of Klansmen, Nazis, and other right-wing thugs with whom they fundamentally disagreed. They worried about the chilling effect that government threats could have on marginally legitimate protests, such as those protected by the *Brandenburg v. Ohio* case in 1969, in which neo-Nazis threatened generalized violence. These concerns seem to have been subordinated to partisan and ideological considerations.

I like Merrick Garland. I supported his nomination to the Supreme Court. And I think he was a good choice for Attorney General. It is in this spirit that I call on him to clarify his memorandum in two respects: (1) by making it clear that law enforcement will not investigate or prosecute raucous protests that fall on the protected side of the Constitutional line; and (2) that whatever standards law enforcement does apply must be applied equally to protests by left-wing agitators.

I stand ready to defend the rights of constitutionally protected protests, regardless of the ideology behind them. I personally approve of masking mandates, with appropriate exceptions, because they can help prevent the spread of a highly contagious virus (see my new book: *The Case for Vaccine Mandates*). I disapprove of teaching captive students from the "critical legal studies" playbook, precisely because it is not critical or objective. It tends to be propaganda rather than education. But I will defend protests against both views with equal vigor, because the First Amendment does not distinguish between protected and unprotected protests based on content, and neither should the Justice Department.

How Social Media Validates Anti-Semitism by Censoring Everything but Anti-Semitism

Social media platforms are engaged in massive censorship of matters related to alleged election fraud, doubts about medicine, vaccination, anything from former president Donald J. Trump, criticism of Black Lives Matter, doubts about transgender activities, climate change, hate speech, and other supposedly politically incorrect tweets and posts. At the same time, it is open season for anti-Semitism, anti-Zionism, and the double standard toward things Jewish.

This combination—censoring many other things but not censoring anti-Semitism—sends a chilling message: If some things are censored because they are *untrue*, then items that are not censored must have passed some test for *truth*. Thus, the hashtag #HitlerWasRight, which has been posted thousands of times across the social media, must be true. So, too, must the thousands of tweets and posts that claim Israel is a genocidal, Nazi state that deliberately murders children. These anti-Semitic posts must also meet the "community standards" of the various social media.

This is a major problem of selective censorship. When you censor nothing, you validate nothing. When you censor some things, then you implicitly validate what you do *not* censor. An example from history will demonstrate the dangers of selective censorship. Back in the day, when the Soviet Union decided what could and could not be read, it put an organization called "Glavlit" in charge of deciding political correctness—people often forget that the very concept of political correctness was invented by Stalin's Soviet Union. I was in Europe debating a Soviet lawyer about anti-Semitism. I presented the audience with illustrations of anti-Semitic material published in the Soviet Union. My opponent outdid me: he presented neo-Nazi material published in the United States that was far worse. He seemed self-satisfied with his one-upmanship. Then I held up the material published in the Soviet Union and asked him to read what it said at the bottom. He understood what I was asking, and he declined to do it. So, I read it out: "Approved by Glavlit." I then read what was on the bottom of the material distributed in the United States. It read "published by the Nazi Party USA."

The audience understood. I won the debate. In the United States, no government agency either censors or approves what is published. Only the Nazi Party was responsible for the hate it disseminated. Whereas in the Soviet Union, the government itself was responsible for the anti-Semitic material that was published. Quite a difference.

The same is quickly becoming true of social media. When they were platforms that allowed everything but illegal material, nothing published on their platforms could be attributed to them. That is why they got the benefit of Section 230, which exempts them from defamation suits: You cannot be responsible for defamation if you do not control what is published on your platform. Now, however, that social media companies have decided to become "Glavlit"—to publish only material that is supposedly truthful and passes its community standards—they have become more like the former Soviet Union than like the United States under the First Amendment.

This is not a call to censor anti-Semitic tweets. It is a call for social media companies to stop censoring other speech based on criteria of supposed truthfulness, "community standards," and other such questionable criteria that are subject to political, ideological, and other biases. I want *no* censorship other than for material that is already prohibited by law. But if the social media companies persist in censoring, they must apply a single standard to everything. They cannot exempt anti-Semitism and false claims against the nation state of the Jewish people—while censoring other supposed "half-truths." If they do, they will be responsible for promoting their own big lie: that everything they do not censor must be true. That is the dilemma of the benevolent censor. The current social media have the worst of both worlds: they censor material that is neither dangerous nor necessarily false; and then permit material which is both highly dangerous and demonstrably false.

The New McCarthyism Comes to Harvard Law School

A recent petition, signed by hundreds of Harvard Law School students and alumni, raises the specter of the new McCarthyism coming to the law school at which I taught for half a century. The petition states that "Harvard Law School faces a choice of whether to welcome the architects and backers of the Trump administration's worse abuses back into polite society." It demands that Harvard not "hire or affiliate with" any of these sinners and threatens that "if it does so the school will be complicit if future attacks on our democracy are even more violent—and more successful."

The petition sees this ban as part of the educational and employment mission of the school: "it would also teach ambitious students of all ages that attempting to subvert the democratic process" will deny them access to the "revolving door to success and prestige." This self-serving defense of censorship is intended to convey a crass economic threat: if you want to get a good job after law school, make sure that Harvard bans teachers and speakers who are trying to "rehabilitate their reputations and obscure the stain of their complicity in the Trump administration. . . ."

This is similar to the message that the original McCarthyites tried to have Harvard convey in the 1950s, when students were denied editorship of the *Law Review*, clerkship recommendations, and other opportunities that they had earned, solely because on their alleged affiliation with Communism and other left-wing causes. One would have thought that current Harvard Law School students would be familiar with the sordid history of McCarthyism that infected many American universities, including Brooklyn College, which I attended as an undergraduate and where I fought against the denial of civil liberties to suspected communists.

One would also think that signatories would be aware that if these vague criteria—anti-democratic, racist, xeno-phobic, and immoral—were applied across the board, they would result in bans on anyone who was associated with the current regimes in China, Cuba, Turkey, Belarus, Russia, Venezuela, the Palestinian Authority, and other repressive governments. It would also apply to supporters of American anti-democratic and anti-free speech groups, such as Antifa, and the very organization—People's Parity Project—that is promoting this anti–free speech petition. Indeed, histori-cally, repression and censorship have been directed primar-ily against the left. Even today, the French government is expressing concern about the impact of "Islamo-leftist" influ-ences from American universities.

The Harvard Law School petition is directed only at Trump supporters, not supporters of left-wing anti-democratic repression, either here or abroad. It is based on the assumption that there is a special "Trump exception" to freedom of speech and due process. But exceptions to free speech and academic freedom for some risk becoming the rule for all.

Free speech for me but for not for thee is not a defensible principle. Today it is the mantra of the new censors, who demand deplatforming and canceling speakers, teachers, and writers who disagree with their anti-Trump zealotry. The voracious appetite of the censor, however, is rarely sated. Some are now trying to silence defenders of the Constitution, such as me, who opposed most of Trump's policies but who also opposed what we believe were unconstitutional efforts to impeach him. When I was invited to speak by a Harvard Law School student group, the event had to be moved off campus as the result of threats to shout me down and silence me.

Much of this effort to exclude Trump supporters from campuses comes from individuals and organizations that also demand more "diversity." But their definition of diversity is limited to race, gender, sexual orientation, and ethnicity. It does not extend to the central mission of universities: to hear and learn from the widest array of views, perspectives, ideologies, and political preferences.

Today's students should welcome Trump supporters and challenge them—respectfully, civilly, and with open minds. They should be willing to listen to views diametrically opposed to their own deeply felt morality and politics. Many of these canceled speakers would express views that are accepted by tens of millions of American voters. Those of us who disagree with these views should feel confident that they will be soundly rejected in the open marketplace of ideas, as they were in the 2020 election. No university or law school should shut down this marketplace, as the old McCarthyism did and as this new McCarthyism is now trying to do. There is no place for selective censorship based on political affiliations at Harvard Law School or any institution of higher education, whether it receives federal funding or not—but especially if it does.

This anti-civil liberties petition should be rejected in the marketplace of ideas by all students, faculty, and administrators who value diversity of opinions both inside and outside the classroom.

The Person or the Constitution? Falsely Charging McConnell with Inconsistency

CNN and other left-wing media went on a rampage after Senator Mitch McConnell delivered his speech explaining why he voted to acquit Donald Trump, despite his belief that Trump had engaged in improper behavior. They accused McConnell of hypocrisy and inconsistency—arguing that if he believed Trump had done wrong, he was obligated to vote for conviction. But it is CNN and the other media that failed to understand the distinction between defending the Constitution and defending the person.

McConnell taught the American people a civics lesson by explaining that the Senate had no constitutional authority to place a former president on trial, even one who had been impeached while still serving in office. In doing so, he echoed a constitutional argument I have been making from the very beginning of this unconstitutional power grab by the Democrat-controlled Congress. The language of the Constitution is clear:

> The President . . . shall be removed from Office on Impeachment for, and Conviction of, Treason, Bribery or other high Crimes and Misdemeanors.

The constitutional power to impeach and remove does not extend beyond federal civil officials who are still in office and can be removed. As James Madison, the father of our Constitution wrote in Federalist 39: "The president of the United States is impeachable at any time during his continuation in office." It is true that once removed, presidents can also be disqualified, but they cannot be disqualified unless they are first removed. The Senators voted by a majority that they had power that the Constitution denied them, but McConnell dissented from that vote along with numerous other Senators, and they acted on their dissenting views in voting to acquit. They were right to do so. That is precisely what happened in the Belknap case, which was cited by the House Managers as a precedent.

The House Managers argued in their brief that the power to impeach is not limited to officials who remain in office but can extend back to any person who held federal office despite how many years ago that person left the office. To have voted to convict citizen Trump would have given Congress a roving commission to seek out and disqualify any potential candidate who ever held federal public office or who might hold office in the future. McConnell correctly rejected that open-ended power grab.

The most important lesson taught by McConnell is that the Constitution protects both the good and the bad, the agreeable and the disagreeable, Republicans and Democrats. One does not have to agree with what President Trump did or said on January 6, in order to correctly conclude that the Senate had no jurisdiction over him once he left office, and that the statements he made—whatever one might think of them—are fully protected by the Constitution.

Back in the bad old days of McCarthyism, anyone who supported the constitutional rights of accused communists was deemed to support communism. That was wrong then, just as it is wrong today to believe that everyone who defends Trump against an unconstitutional impeachment necessarily supports his views or actions. I for one have been quite critical of Trump's actions on January 6 but strongly defend his right to have made his speech even though I think he was wrong to do so. I also defend his right not to be placed on trial as a private citizen by the Senate.

So, three cheers for Mitch McConnell for trying to educate the American public about this important distinction. No cheers for CNN and other left-wing media for returning us to the days of McCarthyism, when these distinctions were deliberately blurred.

To Impeach Biden Now Would Be Unconstitutional

As I predicted when Democrats sought to impeach then-president Donald Trump on unconstitutional grounds, conservative Republicans are planning to try the same unconstitutional gambit now that they have taken control of the House of Representatives. It has been reported that efforts are underway to begin this process.

Rep. Bob Good (R-Va.) has announced: "I have consistently said that President Biden should be impeached for opening our borders and making Americans less safe." Extremist Rep. Marjorie Taylor Greene (R-Ga.) has said through a spokesperson that Joe Biden should have been impeached "as soon as he was sworn in." There are currently several resolutions that have been filed calling for Biden's impeachment on various grounds—none of them constitutional. Now that Republicans have gained control of the House, these and other resolutions are likely to be taken up. They are also planning to impeach several cabinet members, including Attorney General Garland, on unconstitutional grounds.

This was Alexander Hamilton's worst nightmare: that the power to impeach would be weaponized by the party that controls the legislative branch. Here is what Hamilton wrote in *The Federalist Papers*:

> [Impeachment] will seldom fail to agitate the passions of the whole community, and to divide it into parties more or less friendly or inimical to the accused. In many cases it will connect itself with the pre-existing factions, and will enlist all their animosities partialities, influence, and interest on one side or on the other; and in such cases there will always be the greatest danger that the decision will be regulated more by the comparative strength of parties, than by the demonstrations of innocence or guilt.

To prevent that abuse, the Framers limited the grounds for impeachment to treason, bribery, or other high crimes and misdemeanors—not policy differences or even claims of abuse of power or maladministration. But now the criteria seem to be: "because we can"—because we have the votes, regardless of the constitutional criteria.

Both parties are at fault, and they are now playing tit for tat. But two constitutional wrongs do not make a constitutional right. The improper impeachment of Biden should not be used to avenge the improper impeachments of Donald Trump, any more than the impeachments of Donald Trump should have been used to avenge the improper impeachment of Bill Clinton.

The power to impeach a president was extensively debated at the Constitutional Convention. Some argued that there should be no such power. Others argued that it should be broad and include "maladministration." James Madison, the Father of our Constitution, rejected both extremes, the latter because he did not want the president to serve at the pleasure of the legislature. The result was a compromise which permitted impeachment but only for criminal-type behavior akin to treason and bribery—two of the most serious high crimes.

Impeachment of a president was voted only once in the first two centuries of our nation's history. It was regarded as an extreme measure to be used only in cases of real criminality. Now it has become trivialized by both parties in their efforts to gain temporary political advantage, while neglecting the long-term implications for democracy.

I have stood against all such abuse of the Constitution by both parties. In doing so I have stood nearly alone. For the most part, Democrats have favored the impeachment of Republications and the Republications have favored the impeachment of Democrats—without regard to the constitutional criteria. I have opposed all efforts to impeach American presidents, except for Richard Nixon, who resigned under threat of impeachment and removal. Nixon's removal was sought by both parties. He resigned only after Republican leaders told him they would support his impeachment and conviction. That is how it should be. Impeaching a president should receive bipartisan support lest it become a bipartisan weapon as it is becoming now.

So, if Biden were to be impeached, I would defend him with the same vigor with which I defended Trump against an unconstitutional impeachment. Republicans will hate me for this, and Democrats will approve—the exact opposite of how each reacted to my constitutional defense of Trump.

I hope and pray that it will not come to that. Cooler heads among Republican leaders should prevail, as they did not among Democratic leaders in the Trump impeachment or among Republican leaders in the Clinton impeachment. The model should be the proper removal of Richard Nixon for his extensive involvement in serious criminal activities. That standard was not met with Trump, and it is not met with Biden.

Freedom of Speech Includes Freedom to Hear Politically Incorrect Views

There are two distinct but overlapping rights contained within the constitutional right to free speech. The first is the right of the speaker to speak. The second is the right of citizens to hear the views expressed by the speaker. The second may seem implicit in the first, but efforts are now underway to deny citizens the right to hear politically incorrect views expressed by controversial speakers.

Consider the efforts by two Democratic members of Congress to persuade the leading cable and satellite television providers not to carry Fox News or Newsmax. If these coercive efforts were to succeed, Fox and Newsmax would still be allowed to broadcast, but millions of viewers would be denied the right to access them on their televisions.

Or consider "cancel culture," which is intended to punish speakers who have violated some often undefined norm. But it is not only the "guilty" speakers who are punished, but also the innocent audience that is deprived of the right to hear these speakers present their views.

When Manhattan's famed 92nd Street YMHA canceled me because I was falsely accused of having sex with a woman I never met, the real victims of this modern-day McCarthyism were the audience members who wanted to hear me speak in a venue where I have spoken for more than a quarter of a century. The YMHA admitted that it didn't believe the false accusation, but it decided it had to cancel me nonetheless because it "didn't want trouble" from the handful of people who might have protested my appearance.

But what about the hundreds of people who wanted to hear me speak about Israel, but were denied the opportunity to do so? What about their right to listen to me? The protesters, too, have their rights—to refuse to listen to me, and to protest my appearance. But that is not inconsistent with the rights of those who wanted to hear me speak being given that opportunity in the first instance.

The distinction between the right to speak and the right to hear can best be illustrated by reference to a situation that is becoming more common in the age of COVID-19 and Zoom. A foreign speaker who is not a United States citizen has no First Amendment right to speak in the United States. But if he or she is invited to give a Zoom talk by an American audience, that audience has the right to hear the words spoken by that foreigner from a foreign country. There have been several such cases, and I have advocated for the right of the audience to hear speakers whose physical presence has been banned.

Cancel culture directly affects the speakers who are being punished for their purported sins. Among those "canceled" have been some of the world's greatest musicians, such as James Levine and Plácido Domingo. Whether rightly or wrongly, they have been denied the right to perform to audiences that wish to hear them. Anyone has the right to refuse to listen to the music of these canceled performers, but what about the rights of those who have done nothing wrong and who want to simply enjoy their music and art?

If cancel culture is to become American culture, as increasingly appears to be the case, then a balance must be struck among three factors: the due process and free speech rights of the person to be "canceled," the rights of those who wish to hear or see the "canceled" person, and the interests of those who seek the cancellation. This balance should generally be struck in favor of the first two rights because those seeking cancellation have viable alternatives to denying the speakers and listeners their constitutional rights: They can refuse to listen, they can urge others to refuse to listen, they can peacefully protest the speaker, and they can respond to the speaker. What they should not be permitted to do is deny those of us who disagree with cancel culture—or with the cancelation of a particular speaker—the right to decide for ourselves whom we choose to hear.

In a democracy with an open marketplace of ideas, the right to hear is more fundamental than any purported right to cancel.

What Will Happen When the Trump Era Ends?

The Donald Trump era may be nearing its end—though this has been predicted before. Would its end, when it comes, begin to heal our divisions?

Back in the run-up to the 2016 election, Trump exacerbated already palpable divisions within our nation. His first campaign for president was marked by name calling, personal attacks, and exaggerated claims. He won that election fair and square, as I predicted he might in August 2016. I did not support his candidacy, having campaigned for, donated to, and voted for Hillary Clinton. But I accepted the outcome of the election.

The Trump presidency was filled with controversies, from his ban on immigration from designated Muslim countries, to his policies on the Mexican border, to his inconsistencies with regard to COVID-19, and finally to his unwillingness to accept the outcome of the 2020 election.

Whenever the Trump era ends, it may do so with even more division than existed when it began. Trump contributed to that, but so did his enemies. Trump haters demanded that everyone choose sides and pass purity tests. I failed both, refusing to give up my right to assess the president in a nuanced fashion. I opposed many of his policies, but strongly supported his approach to the Middle East peace process. I actively helped his administration in its efforts to achieve peace between Israel and the Palestinians, and normalcy between Israel and its Sunni Arab neighbors. Having opposed President Barack Obama's ill-advised Iran nuclear deal, I supported Trump's tougher approach to Tehran's nuclear ambitions, as well as the movement of the US embassy from Tel Aviv to Jerusalem; I had unsuccessfully urged several previous presidents to make that move. I also supported the Trump administration's decision to recognize Israel's annexation of the Golan Heights, subject to negotiation with Syria in any future peace deal.

Another casualty of the Trump era was the judicial selection process, especially with regard to the Supreme Court. Trump's first two nominations to the High Court were reasonable, though they would not have been my choices. Senator Chuck Schumer's angry threats against the nominations, on the other hand, were unreasonable. The manner in which Democrats and liberals treated Justice Brett Kavanaugh was nothing short of disgraceful, but he was eventually confirmed, if largely along party lines.

Trump's final nomination of Amy Coney Barrett, however, exposed the hypocrisy of Republican Senate leaders who had opposed President Obama's nomination of Merrick Garland eight months before the 2016 election, on the grounds that the next president should make that appointment. When President Trump nominated Barrett less than two months before the 2020 election, the same Republican Senators rushed her through to confirmation, coming up with phony distinctions. Now there are calls to pack the Court with Democratic appointees, and President Biden has appointed a commission to look into the entire process of judicial appointments.

Among the most serious and potentially enduring casualties of the Trump/anti-Trump era was freedom of speech, the press, and assembly. The First Amendment is weaker today than it was when Trump took office. This is largely the fault of anti-Trump zealots, though Trump himself provoked their overreaction by the manner in which he exercised his own freedom of expression. His tweets and other social media statements caused several platforms to ban him and others with whose speech they disagreed. Trump's excesses even provoked traditionally liberal organizations and writers to call for private censorship, emulating tactics they had long condemned as McCarthyite. Trump's second impeachment—based on a speech that most civil libertarians would have found to be protected by the First Amendment had it been delivered by anyone else—damaged the freedom of speech, despite the former president's ultimate acquittal.

From a civil liberties perspective, we are worse off today than we were four years ago. The blame for this decline is shared. Trump provoked his enemies into overreacting against our civil liberties. Those who supported his impeachment tried to create a "Trump exception" to the First Amendment, in response to the "January exception" they feared would be created by failure to impeach him for his incendiary January 6 speech.

The time has come not only to reunite Americans, but to rebuild shattered friendships and to move forward with malice toward none and charity for all. The time has also come to re-strengthen our civil liberties, most especially our First Amendment rights. Now that Trump is no longer president, I hope fair-weather civil libertarians who were willing to compromise our rights in the interests of getting Trump will come to their senses and understand that those constitutional rights are more important than any president and must endure beyond any presidency.

Trump Must Condemn Ye More Strongly

Whenever I met with then President Trump, he would ask me why more Jews don't vote for him. He emphasized his role in moving the embassy to Jerusalem, recognizing the Golan Heights as part of Israel, and combatting anti-Semitism on campuses. I explained that although many Jews appreciated his positive role on these important issues, most Jews vote on a range of issues, including choice, gay rights, climate, guns, separation of church and state, and the Supreme Court.

Now I would have to add to that explanation for why many Jews will not vote for him: the recent very public meal Trump had with two overt anti-Semites, Ye (Kanye West) and Nick Fuentes. Many Jews take him at his word that he was unaware that Fuentes was a Holocaust denier and Jew hater. But Trump had to be aware of recent, highly publicized anti-Jewish statements by Ye, especially his frightening call for "death con 3" against the Jewish people.

Why then would Trump agree to associate with such an anti-Semite? Trump himself is not an anti-Semite. His record with respect to Jews has been quite good. It is true that Ye had praised him on the Tucker Carlson show, and we know that he appreciates and rewards praise. But that is no excuse for a public display of friendship toward a bigot. He could have thanked him in private. David Duke has praised him too, as have other horrible people. Trump would never be seen in public with Duke and his ilk. So why is Ye different?

Defenders of Trump point out that Ye is crazy and that his anti-Semitism is a product of his sick paranoia. That is no excuse for legitimating Ye by dining with him in a very public way, especially in the immediate aftermath of his "death con" threat.

Trump should now go out his way to delegitimate Ye and his dangerous, even if crazy, calls for "death con 3," as well his anti-Semitic canards about Jewish control over Black people and others. Whether crazy, bigoted, or both, Ye has an enormous following on social and other media. He must be discredited in the court of public opinion, especially by a former president who credited him among his own millions of followers and admirers.

Trump must do more—much more—to use his bully pulpit to try to undo the terrible damage he has done by dining with Ye and Fuentes. This is not a partisan or "Get Trump" demand. It comes from Jews and non-Jews who have supported him, befriended him, voted for him, and honored him. His former ambassador to Israel, the Prime Minister designate of Israel, the head of the Zionist organization of America, and many other friends have critiqued him and asked him to make amends. He should do so—strongly, unequivocally, loudly, unambiguously, and immediately. He made a serious mistake, and he should be big enough to admit it, even if it costs him some votes among Ye followers. This is not about votes—by Jews or others. It is a matter of basic principle and decency.

At a time of increasing anti-Semitism from both hard right and hard left, as well as from some Islamic extremists, every decent person, regardless of race, party, ideology, or other identities, must come together to discredit the oldest of prejudices that only seems to increase and spread with the passage of time. Trump should continue to be part of the solution to that ancient problem—rather than becoming part of the problem. His legitimation of Ye may encourage others to emulate his bigotry. Trump now has a special responsibility to delegitimate him among his many followers.

Trump Calls for Termination of Constitutional Rules

Former president Trump recently stated that the massive fraud that he believes occurred in the 2020 election "allows for termination of all rules . . . even those found in the Constitution." This is a dangerous and unprecedented statement by a former and possibly future president. When Trump took office in 2017, he swore to "preserve, protect and defend the Constitution." If he were to be elected again in 2024, he would be required, under the Constitution, to take the same oath. That oath makes no exception for claims about an unfair or even fraudulent election. There are mechanisms for challenging elections <u>under</u> the Constitution. Indeed, Trump sought to employ his interpretation of the Constitution when he tried, unsuccessfully, to get Vice President Pence to reject the electoral votes of certain states. He also engaged in constitutionally protected speech when he made his ill-advised January 6 talk. But now he seems to suggest that it would be permissible to act outside of the Constitution to challenge his electoral defeat.

Let us never forget that the only reason Trump was elected president in 2016 was because of the Constitution. He lost the popular vote by a considerable majority. He became president <u>only</u> because the very Constitution he would undermine provided for presidents to be elected by the votes of the electoral college rather than direct popular votes. Taking Trump's dangerous argument to its logical or illogical conclusion would permit Hillary Clinton to have called for the termination of constitutional rules in order to affect the will of voters, a substantial majority of whom cast their ballots for her.

Trump can't have it both ways. He can't depend on the Constitution to win an election and then seek to terminate the Constitution when he loses an election. The United States Constitution is the oldest surviving written constitution in history. It has survived crises, both internal and external. It has an amendment process by which its provisions can be changed, and new provisions added. What it does not have is a provision for terminating it if a presidential candidate is dissatisfied with the results of an election.

If Trump were able to terminate the Constitution at will, then other presidents or losing candidates could do the same. This would mark the end of the rule of constitutional law which has served our country so well over the years. Our Constitution is not perfect. Its origin was in compromises, some of them deeply immoral. It was not written for a democracy, but rather for a Republic. Indeed, many of its key provisions are anti-democratic. They include the Electoral College, the Senate, and an appointed judiciary with the power to overrule the elected branches. Today many on the hard left are advocating termination or ignoring what they regard as an anachronistic document written by slave-owning men. Now the leader of the right wing seems to be joining that call. The combination of hard left and hard right calls to terminate the Constitution enhance the possibility that this movement may become more mainstream.

Throughout history, there have been calls for termination of the Constitution. In the beginning, critics called it a "godless Constitution." Abolitionists called it a slave owners Constitution. Following the enactment of the post-Civil War amendments, many southerners regarded the Constitution as "victors justice," really injustice. During the New Deal, many Democrats saw it as a barrier to economic and social progress. During the Civil Rights movement, many southerners accused it of destroying their way of life. Now, radical and woke academics see it as a barrier to their utopias. It is against this historical background that Trump's ill-advised statement must be considered. America is a centrist country that has traditionally marginalized both the hard right and the hard left. Americans have rejected past efforts to terminate the Constitution, while accepting amendments and judicial interpretations that make it relevant to contemporary concerns. The Constitution "ain't broke," and we should not scuttle it. Nor should we pack the courts in a partisan manner. The rule of law requires that all Americans comply with the Constitution. No one is above the law and certainly no one is above the Constitution.

The "Get Trump" Campaign's Best Ally: Donald Trump

The "Get Trump at any cost" campaign is picking up steam following Trump's announcement that he will run in 2024. The campaigners include those who advocate legal means, such as aggressive electoral, media, and economic tactics. They also include some who advocate constitutionally questionable or even plainly illegal means, such as disqualifying him under the 14th Amendment, stretching criminal statutes to cover non-criminal conduct, and going after his lawyers and other alleged "facilitators."

Then there is Donald Trump himself, who seems determined to give his enemies ammunition that can be used in the campaign against him. Many of his recent actions and statements have not only given aid and comfort to his opponents; they have turned longtime friends and supporters against him. These unforced errors may not be enough to destroy his candidacy, but they have certainly weakened him.

His very public meal with two overt anti-Semites—Ye and Nick Fuentes—have hurt his standing among many Jewish supporters. So have several recent statements stereotyping Jews and suggestion that they do, or should, have more loyalty to "their country" Israel, than to the United States

His confusing claim that the alleged fraud in the 2020 election would justify "the termination of all rules . . . even those found in the Constitution" has alienated many conservative strict constructionists. His enthusiastic support for so many losing candidates in the 2022 mid-term elections has diminished the values of his endorsements. Even his opposition to the prisoner exchange that brought home WNBA star Brittany Griner has drawn mixed reaction from his base.

These are all unforced errors that seem more to be products of his uncontrollable impulses than of any calculated effort to increase his chances of winning. They certainly don't seem to have helped his electoral prospects.

Donald Trump is a complex paradox. He is not personally an anti-Semite or a bigot. Those labels simply don't fit, though they certainly fit some of his followers who use his actions and statements to validate their own hateful opinions. Trump doesn't seem to understand or care that he influences and validates some very bad people and some very dangerous views. For example, he dined with Ye not because of Ye's anti-Semitism, but despite it. Trump was rewarding him for the positive things he said about him on the Tucker Carlson show, ignoring the negative implications of this very public reward.

Trump's objectionable stereotyping of Jews—good negotiators, real estate developers, media controllers, and Israel lovers—were actually intended by him to be flattering but are seen by anti-Semites as evidence of undue Jewish influence and power.

Trump seems insensitive to the negative influence he inadvertently exerts. That is not a justification or excuse for his wrongful actions, but it may help to explain what otherwise seems inexplicable, especially to those who know him.

During the 2016 campaign, many pundits predicted that his repeated gaffes—about women, Senator McCain, soldiers, reporters, and others—would surely sink his candidacy. It didn't. Part of the reason is that the 2016 election presented a choice of negatives for many voters, especially those who hated Hillary Clinton more than they disliked Donald Trump. It's different now. Trump's negatives are very high and climbing. His recent shenanigans are unlikely to reduce them.

What may well help him, despite his self-destructive mindset, are the unfair, unethical, illegal, and unconstitutional means being used to "get" him by some radical opponents who care more about the ends they seek—preventing Trump from running—than they do about the dangerous means they are employing. Many centrist Americans react badly to unfair tactics that target political opponents for special negative treatment. Trump understands this and uses the unfairness directed at him to rally and expand his base.

These unfair means also keep Trump front and center in the news, which he needs to keep his candidacy viable. Accordingly, those who want to prevent Trump from retaking the White House would be well advised to stop using unlawful and unfair means to "get" him, and to let him "get" himself, which he seems entirely capable of doing by his own lack of control.

The Most Transformative Events of the Twenty-First Century

Which events most transformed our nation during the first twenty-two years of this century? Five stand out. Each was utterly unpredictable and largely unpreventable. They changed the course of our history, our ideology, our attitudes, and our responses. They will have a continuing impact on our lives for years to come.

In roughly chronological order they are as follows:

1) The attack on the World Trade Center and Pentagon on 9/11/2001
2) The election of Donald Trump on November 8, 2016
3) The COVID pandemic starting in early 2020
4) The killing of George Floyd on May 25, 2020
5) The Russian attack against Ukraine on February 24, 2022

Some observers may add other events, but few can deny the centrality of these five, though there may be arguments about the order of their significance. I will offer my own views on that question, but first a description of the impact of each.

The 9/11 attack shook our nation to its core and displayed our vulnerability to asymmetrical warfare from small groups capable of turning our own "weapons" against us to inflict enormous damage. It provoked wars in Iraq and Afghanistan with considerable casualties and not a lot to show for them. It destabilized the Mideast and strengthened Iran and its proxies in Iraq and Lebanon. Although we killed or captured many of the perpetrators, we did so with an enduring cost to civil liberties and the rule of law, as exemplified by Guantanamo and The Patriot Act. It has now been more than two decades since that fateful day and its impact on our collective psyche persists.

The election of Donald Trump on November 8, 2016, divided Americans more than any election since Lincoln defeated John C. Breckinridge in 1860. Although Trump's election did not cause a civil war, it resulted in the breakup of families, friendships, and party affiliations. It also caused a breakdown of communications, a reduction of nuance, and a demand that everyone choose sides and be absolutely loyal to their side. It damaged civil liberties and the rule of law in two ways: First, Trump himself undercut these pillars of democracy by playing fast and loose with the Constitution; and second, his opponents were willing to compromise constitutional rights in their efforts to "get" him. Even organizations long dedicated to civil liberties, such as the ACLU, were prepared to compromise their principles to prevent what they regarded as an even greater threat to liberty—namely Trump. The end result is a nation with fewer fundamental rights and greater dangers to our liberty.

COVID came out of the blue—or China. No one can be sure of its source. We can be sure of its consequences. America and much of the rest of the world was shut down and there were many deaths and considerable illness. My mother nearly died during the flu epidemic of 1917. I lived through the polio scare of the 1950s. Smallpox was so rampant during the revolutionary war that General Washington mandated that all troops be inoculated. But there were no shutdowns like the ones we experienced during 2020–21. The impact on schooling, workplace absences, and business was incalculable. But owing to the rapid response, the development of vaccines and treatment, and the widespread wearing of masks, the damage was contained. We still suffer, however, from the aftereffects, both physical and psychological. We are also still experiencing the political repercussions of the highly divisive steps that were taken.

The killing of George Floyd on May 25, 2020 changed the way Americans look at race. The brutality of the policeman who caused the death of this forty-six-year-old Black man symbolized for many Americans our sordid history of police violence toward Black men and women and resulted in a broad reckoning about the role of race in our nation. Virtually every institution was impacted by this reckoning, ranging from politics to the media to education to culture to advertising to corporate board rooms to sports and to interpersonal relations and attitudes. Rarely in our history has one event—which in years past would have been ignored—had so profound and persuasive an impact on the lives of so many Americans of all races, genders, ages, and socioeconomic backgrounds. It is difficult to think of any aspect of American life that has not been impacted by this horrible killing and its aftermath. People may differ as to the bene-fits and costs of specific changes, but no one can doubt the pervasiveness of this reckoning on our national character, attitudes, and actions.

Finally, there is the continuing Russian assault on Ukraine. Although Russia is clearly at fault, even this issue divides Americans, at least to some degree, espite its lack of direct impact on our people. It has shattered the long-time peace of Eastern Europe. No one knows how and when it will end and what its implications will be for the world order.

These then are the five events that have most shaped the first twenty-two years of this century. They have in common that none was entirely predictable or preventable. Accordingly, it was difficult to prepare for them and their consequences. Our responses were ad hoc and reactive. Hopefully, we learned lessons that might help us respond more effectively to the unpredictable future threats we will inevitably face during the rest of this century.

My personal choice for the most transformative event for Americans: the killing of George Floyd and the widespread racial reckoning that followed. It profoundly altered the role of race in nearly every aspect of American life. It made us more race conscious and ended MLK's dream of a color-blind society in which people are judged by the content of their character, rather than the color of their skin. The legacy of George Floyd is a world of identity politics based largely on race. For some Americans this is an entirely positive devel-opment. For others it also has negative implications. But no American is entirely immune from its effects. Hence my first-place vote.

January 6 Committee Referral Violated
Unconstitutional Separation of Powers

The January 6 Committee has voted to refer former president Donald Trump to the Justice Department for possible criminal prosecution. This referral violates both the letter and spirit of the Constitution for at least two reasons.

First, Article 1 of the Constitution grants Congress "all legislative powers" and only "legislative powers." Under our system of separation of powers, the power to prosecute lies exclusively with the executive branch through the Justice Department. Congress has no authority to refer specific individuals for prosecution. It is beyond the scope of its constitutional authority.

Second, Congress is specifically denied the power to pass any "bill of attainder."

Prior to America's independence, the British Parliament enacted such bills that prosecuted named individuals. Our Constitution prohibited Congress from prosecuting named individuals. The power of Congress is limited to passing laws of general application that can be applied to specific individuals only by the Justice Department and a grand jury. A congressional committee officially voting to refer a named individual for prosecution violates the spirit of the explicit prohibition against congressional bills of attainder.

There is one possible exception to this separation of powers limitation on naming individuals. Section 5 of the 14th Amendment gives Congress the power "to enforce, by appropriate legislation" the provisions of that amendment, which include the disqualification from holding federal office anyone who "has engaged in insurrection or rebellion" against the United States or "given aid or comfort to the enemies thereof." Section 3 gives it the power to "remove such disability" by a two-thirds vote of each house. This is a very limited power intended to apply to southern rebels during the Civil War, as evidenced by the specific reference to "the loss or emancipation of any slave" in Section 5. But even if it were deemed applicable to the events of January 6, 2021, the recent referral was not made pursuant to that amendment. Indeed, it was not made pursuant to any provision of the Constitution, because there is none that would authorize it.

The Justice Department will politely accept the referral and then place it in a file that is round and sits on the floor. A special prosecutor has already been appointed and is conducting a thorough and hopefully objective investigation. The Justice Department really doesn't need a referral from Congress, nor should it pay any attention to it.

The Committee itself was composed of both Democrat and Republican kangaroos. The two "Republicans" were selected by Democrats. The Republicans originally appointed by the Republican minority leader were vetoed by Speaker Nancy Pelosi in violation of the traditions of the House of Representatives. The Republicans then refused to choose two other members, so the Democrats selected them. They served only as cover for the one-sided investigation, report, and referrals. The Committee's proceedings were more like a show trial—complete with slickly presented videos—than a serious legislative hearing in aid of passing laws. It was reminiscent of a Democratic version of Republican McCarthyism back in the 1950s, where citizens were named and put on blacklists.

The so-called January 6 Committee was the culmination of the "Get Trump" efforts that ignored constitutional constraints and the rule of law. It may not be the last word, however, since there is always the possibility that the special prosecutor may indict. If he does, it won't be because of the congressional referral, it will be because the Justice Department's investigation independently produced compelling evidence of criminal conduct. It will also be, hopefully, because experienced prosecutors made prosecutorial decisions based on Justice Department standards, priorities, and the exercise of discretion, not based on partisan advantage.

Charging a presidential candidate with a crime is as serious as it gets, especially if he is running against the incumbent who controls the Justice Department. If not done properly and objectively, it is the stuff of banana republics. As one South American dictator once put it: "for my friends everything; for my enemies the law!"

The ill-advised congressional referral will make it more difficult to prosecute Trump without it appearing partisan. The committee report and referrals will taint the special prosecutor's decision in the mind of many who will believe, even erroneously, that it was influenced by the corrupt committee process.

This is a good lesson on the centrality of our separation of powers to our system of governance. It is an important reminder of why congressional committees should stay out of prosecutorial decisions and criminal referrals.

Is There a Legal Remedy for Santos's Lies?

Congressman George Santos has lived a life of lies. He has lied about his early life, his academic record, his business experience, his wealth, his heritage, his personal life, and his criminal record. He is fortunate that the vast majority of these lies have not been under oath. Nor have they defamed specific individuals. Unless he has lied on government forms, it is unlikely that he can be successfully prosecuted or civilly sued. His victims are primarily the voters who cast ballots for a person who was very different from who they believed him to be.

It is possible therefore that George Santos will not be held legally accountable for his lies, especially the most egregious ones which got him nominated and elected to Congress.

Some will be surprised to learn that the First Amendment to the Constitution protects most lies. It allows anti-Semites to deny the Holocaust. It protects sexists and racists from mendaciously engaging in false and malicious hate speech. It does not allow Congress to enact laws protecting the memory of soldiers who died in defense of our country. It allows ignorant people to claim that the earth is flat and that astronauts never landed on the moon.

Although lying when not under oath and when not attacking a specific individual is not a crime in America, it is in other countries that punish the falsification of history and hate speech directed at groups rather than individuals. We have chosen a different way that is not without costs. Pervasive falsity in the public arena is the price we pay for freedom of speech and the marketplace of ideas.

The dangers of punishing general falsehoods are demonstrated by the laws of other countries. In Poland it is a crime to state that the Polish people participated in the Holocaust, although that statement is absolutely true as a matter of history. Polish people not only collaborated with Nazis, some continued to kill Jews even after the Nazis left. The Polish parliament has declared the historic truth to be a punishable lie. When I went to Poland several years ago to help commemorate the end of Nazism, I deliberately challenged that law by directly stating in a public meeting that many Polish people participated in the Holocaust (though many did not). I was not arrested.

In Turkey, it is a crime to claim that the Armenian genocide occurred. In France it is a crime to deny that this very same event occurred.

It is for historians, not judges or juries, to determine the truth or falsity of historic claims, just as it is the job of scientists to pass on the accuracy of scientific claims.

Over the past several years, there have been false claims about COVID, vaccines, and other medical issues. Lying about such matters can cause significant harm.

Significant harm can also be caused by false claims regarding elections. In Brazil such claims about the most recent election contributed to violence. In our own country, false claims about the 2020 presidential election have exacerbated divisions among our citizens.

Allowing George Santos to live his life of lies without legal accountability is the heavy price we pay for denying the government the power to censor. What Winston Churchill once said about democracy can be paraphrased to apply to freedom of speech: the worst policy, except for all the others that have been tried over time.

The alternative to freedom of speech is necessarily some form of censorship. Throughout history, censorship by governments, churches, and other powerful institutions has been the rule. It has not worked. Nor has untrammeled free speech worked perfectly. But history has clearly demonstrated that censorship is far more dangerous to liberty than is free speech. Thomas Jefferson may have overstated it when he wrote the following in a letter twenty-five years after the Declaration of Independence: "[W]e have nothing to fear from the demoralizing reasoning of some, if others are left free to demonstrate their errors. . . ." He was surely correct, however, that as long as truth tellers are able to respond to liars, we have far more to fear from censorship than from free speech.

So let's continue to condemn George Santos in the court of public opinion but let's not criminalize his lies, unless they fall within narrow exceptions.

Death of Nuance in Politics and the Media

We are experiencing the death of nuanced discourse in many parts of the world today. Instead, we see black or white debate between two sides, each insisting that they are right and the other wrong in every respect. Neither side is willing to give intellectual quarter to the other or even to listen to their counter arguments. Unconditional surrender is demanded. Compromise is unthinkable in this war of ideologies.

Gone are days when friends could disagree and yet respect each other's views. Today long-term friendships end over an unwillingness to acknowledge that there may be two sides to a divisive issue. Counter arguments are not answered by facts or logic but by ad hominem insults.

Two current examples will illustrate this degrading of discourse. The first involves the disclosure that both Donald Trump and Joe Biden mishandled classified material after they left office. The good news is that virtually all Americans agree on one thing: that there are important and dispositive differences that make one case far more serious than the other. The bad news is that half the country is sure that Trump's is worse, while the other half is certain that Biden's is worse. No one seems to believe that there are some issues that make Trump's worse, while there are others that make Biden's worse. For most, it's black and white. One of them did everything wrong, while the other did nothing wrong. Case closed.

The second example of lack of nuance involves the debates here and in Israel about the role and influence of the Supreme Court. Here, the hard left wants to weaken the current Supreme Court by packing it with enough new justices to move it leftward. In Israel, the right wants to weaken its high court by allowing the legislature to override its liberal decisions and by giving the conservative legislature more of a role in selecting the justices.

Left-wing Israelis are taking to the street in mass protests against these judicial "reforms," claiming they will bring an end to Israel as a democracy. Supporters claim they will enhance democracy by transferring power from an unelected elitist court to a Knesset elected by the majority.

Each side has a point. Courts are supposed to be checks on democracy and protectors of minorities and often unpopular civil liberties. When the courts rule in favor of minorities over majorities, pure democracy is compromised, but it is compromised in the interest of fundamental civil liberties and human rights for all. The goal is to strike the appropriate balance between majority and minority rights. This requires nuance, calibration, and a willingness to compromise—precisely the elements that are quickly disappearing from political, media, and academic dialogue.

Both in Israel and here, opponents of the only "correct" approach—and according to them there is only one correct approach— are subjected to ad hominem attacks, called fascist, and canceled. Demonization has replaced dialogue. Both countries are the poorer for it.

The great American jurist Learned Hand correctly observed that the spirit of liberty is "the spirit which is not too sure that it is right." Certainty and intolerance of opposing views are the hallmarks of intellectual tyranny that easily morph into political tyranny. If one is certain of the absolute correctness of his views, he often sees no need for the right to dissent or the need for due process. We are seeing that today among many in the "woke" generation who believe that their noble ends justify ignoble means, such as shutting down debate and denying due process to those accused of politically incorrect sins or crimes. On the hard right, we have always seen intolerance and now increasing violence— justified in the name of preserving traditional American values.

The road to political hell is indeed paved with certainty that one's intentions are good. Or as the great Justice Louis Brandeis taught us a century ago, "the greatest dangers to Liberty lurk in the insidious encroachment by men of zeal but without understanding."

Today, not only is nuance not welcome in most political dialogue, it is punished. Those deemed guilty of compromising the narrative by introducing nuance are regarded as traitors to the cause and attacked, cancelled, or shunned. Others, who by their nature are open to compromise, are discouraged from participating in the discussion.

The end result is the zero-sum games that are being played out in the conflicts over the dual mishandling of classified information, and the attacks on the Supreme

Court. The debates over these important issues have been considerably dumbed down by the extremism and lack of nuance by both sides.

Republicans Want to Impeach Mayorkas on Grounds They Rejected in Trump's Case

The story sounds familiar: The party in control of the House of Representatives wants to impeach a political opponent on grounds not specified in the Constitution. In the current case, the Republican speaker of the House is seeking to impeach Democratic Homeland Security Secretary Alejandro Mayorkas on the ground that he is "derelict" in his duties. When the Democrats controlled the House, they initially impeached President Trump on the equally vague and unconstitutional ground that he had "abused his power."

When the Democrats went after Trump, Republicans insisted that the only permissible grounds were "treason, bribery, or other high crimes and misdemeanors," as specified in the Constitution. Now that the shoe is on the other foot, many of these same Republicans are claiming that "dereliction" of duty is enough.

So too with Democrats who insisted that "abuse" was sufficient to impeach Trump, but now they are saying that for Mayorkas, the Constitution requires high crimes and misdemeanors, not mere dereliction.

These inconsistencies are apparent for all to see, but apparently irrelevant to partisan hypocrites who don't care. They interpret the Constitution one way for their enemies and another way for their friends. Rights for me but not for thee!

Alexander Hamilton warned, in *The Federalist Papers*, that the "greatest danger" of impeachment is that it will be used politically and will turn on the number of votes each party could secure, "that the decision will be regulated more by the comparative strength of parties, than by the real demonstration of innocence or guilt."

For the first two hundred years of our nation's existence, this was merely an abstract threat. But since the ill-advised impeachment of President Bill Clinton, Hamilton's nightmare has become a reality. Clinton was impeached for personal acts that fell far short of the constitutional criteria.

Democratic supporters of Clinton, including me, insisted that the constitutional criteria had not been met and that Clinton's impeachment was a mere assertion of political power rather than a principal application of the Constitution. Republicans responded that Clinton had disgraced the presidency by his private conduct, and that this was enough to impeach. Ultimately Clinton was acquitted by the Senate.

Then the Democrats tried to get even by twice impeaching Donald Trump for conduct that did not meet the constitutional criteria. I argued against Trump's removal at the first Senate trial. Trump was twice acquitted by the Senate.

At the time of Trump's impeachment, I predicted that when the Republicans took control of the House of Representatives, they would play tit for tat. That prediction has, unfortunately, come true. Immediately upon the election of Joe Biden, some Republicans called for his impeachment. That failed to generate widespread support among the Republican base. Now they are aiming at the Secretary of Homeland Security, who was appointed by Biden. The Republicans who support his impeachment know full well that they cannot succeed in removing him by a two-thirds Senate vote. But they still want to impeach him in order to highlight the alleged failures of this administration in controlling the southern border. They may have enough Republican votes to achieve this unconstitutional political goal, despite the fact that some Republican moderates seem unwilling to go along with this charade.

This is what it has come to. Both parties are willing to weaponize the constitutional criteria for impeachment in order to achieve political benefits. The leaders and many members of both parties seem willing to apply the Constitution in a partisan manner—exactly the opposite of what was intended by the Framers. Winning is their only goal, and to achieve that partisan end, all unconstitutional means are acceptable, as long as they have the votes.

This dual distortion of the Constitution endangers all Americans by substituting the role of power for the rule of law. Decent politicians on both sides should refuse to play this unconstitutional game of tit for tat and should demand compliance with the text of the Constitution. But don't count on decency from politicians. There are too few profiles in courage or consistency among today's House members. We can only hope there are enough of them to prevent the impeachment of Mayorkas on unconstitutional grounds. There were not enough to prevent the unconstitutional impeachments of Clinton and Trump. Things may have changed since then, but not for the better.

The Supreme Court Leaker Must Be Found

The Supreme Court has released the findings of its investigation into who leaked the draft decision overruling *Roe v. Wade*. The investigation failed to discover the leaker, and the matter now seems to be closed.

This is an unsatisfactory resolution to one of the most serious breaches of confidentiality in American history.

Let us not underestimate the seriousness of this leak. It apparently encouraged a potential assassin to try to kill Justice Brett Kavanaugh in an effort to change the outcome of the case. It could easily have succeeded in doing so.

The failure to discover the leaker will encourage others to engage in actions which they believe are well-intentioned civil disobedience. The mystery of who leaked this draft decision must be solved.

The investigation done by the Supreme Court was destined to failure. It was put in the hands of the Courts' marshal whose job it is to protect the justices and to assure order in the Supreme Court building. The office of the marshal is not equipped to conduct difficult investigations. The matter should have been turned over to the FBI, or a special counsel appointed by the Justice Department, as was done with the unauthorized possession of classified material by President Biden and former president Trump.

Let's be clear about one thing: the improper disclosure of the Supreme Court draft opinion in this case was at least as serious a breach as the Biden or Trump violations. Neither Biden or Trump disclosed any classified material or actually endangered the security of the United States. They were dangerous because of the potential improper disclosure, whereas the Supreme Court leak involved an actual disclosure that impacted the High Court in numerous negative ways.

President Trump criticized the Supreme Court investigation, arguing that the reporter who published the draft opinion should have been subpoenaed and threatened with imprisonment if they did not disclose the source. Such compulsion would violate the journalist-source privilege that exists in many jurisdictions. It is not an absolute privilege as evidenced by the fact that journalists, most famously Judith Miller of the *New York Times*, actually spent time in prison for refusing to comply with judicial orders to disclose their source. Subpoenaing a journalist and threatening her with imprisonment should be a last resort, but it is possible. (see pages 164–166)

Would it be justified in this case? Perhaps. The likelihood is that, like Judith Miller, the journalist who received and published the draft opinion would refuse to disclose its source, although no one ever knows what impact the threat of imprisonment would have on a given journalist.

The journalist him or herself was not at fault for publishing the draft opinion. It was highly newsworthy, and like the Pentagon Papers, and other confidential materials that have been published, the journalists receiving them have an obligation of disclosure to the public.

The same cannot be said about the Supreme Court employee who violated his or her commitment to confidentiality, by improperly disclosing a document that was supposed to be kept secret until the decision was rendered by the justices. If the source or sources are finally identified, they will probably defend their actions on the basis of a higher good. But noble ends do not justify improper or unethical means, especially if the disclosure might well have threatened innocent life.

So do not allow the investigation to end with this report. Thus far, the entire matter has been relegated to the judicial branch, because that is the one most directly affected. But all Americans are the victims of this breach, and both the executive and legislative branches have default roles to play if the Supreme Court cannot do the job properly.

Despite the fact that disclosure in and of itself may not be a crime, it may involve criminal conduct either before, during, or after the disclosure itself. The FBI certainly has jurisdiction to investigate whether a crime has been committed.

Congress too may have an appropriate role in assuring that this breach does not recur. The report issued by the investigators faulted the security at the High Court. That problem won't be easy to solve because law clerks work on drafts and often take them home. The investigation also disclosed that several law clerks told their wives or partners about the decision.

I was a law clerk in the Supreme Court sixty years ago, when each justice had only two law clerks and there were far fewer personnel in the institution. The first two months of my clerkship the doors of the Supreme Court were open to anyone. A visitor could simply knock at the justices' doors and ask for an appointment. Then in the third month of my clerkship President Kennedy was assassinated. I was the one who told the justices, who were in confidential session at the time, of this tragedy. Nearly everything changed following the assassination. Security was enhanced, barriers were erected, and access to the justices was severely limited. But nothing was done to protect the secrecy of draft opinions, and I suspect that little or nothing has been done since.

It will not be cost-free to impose restrictions on law clerk access to and handling of draft opinions. That cost, provoked by the current breach, may be worth incurring in order to protect future disclosures.

The Case for Compelling the Journalist to Disclose the Source of the Supreme Court Leak

When the marshal of the Supreme Court issued her report concluding that her eight-month investigation failed to uncover the source of the leak, former president Trump demanded that the reporters who published the draft opinion in the Barns case be compelled to reveal their source.

There are several problems with this demand. First, the marshal's office does not have the authority to compel reporters to testify. It could, however, seek the aid of the Justice Department, which does have the power to seek grand jury subpoenas to investigate possible crimes. Although it is not a crime to leak confidential Supreme Court documents, it is a crime to lie about it to the marshal's office or in an affidavit. And if the source was among those questioned, he or she must have lied. Whether or not there was a crime, the House Judiciary Committee could investigate the leak and issue subpoenas to the journalists. A Republican controlled committee would have a political incentive to carry out Trump's demand. Thus, the procedural barrier to finding an institution that has the power to compel can be overcome.

The substantive barrier—whether any government institution can compel a journalist to reveal sources—raises a potentially more daunting problem, since these journalists will surely refuse to disclose who gave them the draft opinion based on the journalist-source privilege. A court would have to decide whether to compel the disclosure. The judge would begin with the proposition that the journalist-source privilege is not absolute, as the Judith Miller case will attest. That distinguished former *New York Times* journalist served eighty-five days in jail for refusing to divulge the source for her investigation into a leak that identified a covert CIA agent. Other journalists as well have been compelled to reveal their sources when the legitimate governmental interest in the source being disclosed was deemed to outweigh the legitimate journalistic interest in protecting it.

So, what are the strengths and weaknesses of the countervailing interests in this case? The public has a great interest in sources revealing and the media publishing secrets about official misconduct or questionable actions that the government seeks to suppress. The Pentagon Papers and some of what was published by Wikileaks may fit into this category. (I provided legal counsel in both those cases.)

Contrast those cases to the Supreme Court leak. What legitimate public interest was served by the wrongful disclosure of the draft opinion months before it was scheduled to be released? What legitimate end was the source intending to achieve by the early disclosure? I can think of several illegitimate goals: improperly influencing justices—either way—who might be wavering and subject to legitimate persuasion by fellow justices. This is a realistic possibility since we now know that Chief Justice Roberts was lobbying one or two justices to join his concurring opinion which fell short of overturning *Roe*. If the source favored overruling, he or she may have believed that disclosing the draft and vote would lock in the justices who had joined the preliminary opinion. If the source opposed overruling, they may have believed that the negative public reaction to the leaked result could have changed the mind of a justice. Either way, that was an impermissible goal: justices are not supposed to be influenced by this kind of pressure.

The most extreme and unlikely end sought by the source may have been to incentivize a violent opponent of overruling to try to alter the vote by assassinating a swing justice. Unlikely as it is that this was the intent, it came close to being the result when shortly after the leak a potential assassin was captured near Justice Brett Kavanaugh's home armed with lethal weapons.

Even if no legitimate purpose was served by this particular leak, some would argue that compelling the journalist to reveal this source might discourage other sources from disclosing really important information about ongoing government misconduct.

Another argument is that compelling disclosure would be futile, since all decent journalists would do what Miller did: go to jail rather that break her promise of confidentiality. Maybe. But some journalists have complied with court orders to disclose or go to prison. No one can know for sure whether these journalists would become martyrs for the privilege or put their own interests first until they are put to the difficult choice.

In any event both these arguments go too far. They would require an absolute privilege that would deny the courts the power to compel Miller and other journalists who were held in contempt. But the privilege, in most jurisdictions, is not absolute; it requires judges to weigh the costs and benefits of compelling disclosure.

A fair weighing by a court would conclude that this is a close case. If either side had a presumption in its favor, it might tip the balance. But in the absence of a presumption either way, the case for compelled disclosure has a slight advantage, because of the uniqueness of this case: The source here did not seek to expose any wrongdoing by the government, but only the usual workings of the Supreme Court, weeks before they were supposed to be made public. The only wrong that would be exposed here was by the source. A court may well conclude that the public's right to know who the leaker was outweighs the need to protect this wrong-doing source.

The Important Line between Civil and Criminal Is Being Breached

There are two fundamental mechanisms of justice for wrongs committed. The first is civil, in which the wrong is compensated economically—by the payment of money. The second is criminal, in which the wrongdoer is punished—by imprisonment, probation, or fine.

Our constitution recognizes this historic distinction by guaranteeing different rights in civil and criminal cases. The Bill of Rights provides that "in all criminal prosecutions" a plethora of important procedural protections must be accorded the defendant. These include a "speedy and public trial by an impartial jury," "the assistance of counsel," the ability to confront adverse witnesses and call favorable ones, prohibitions against compelled self-incrimination and double jeopardy, reasonable bail, and no "cruel and unusual punishment."

In civil cases, on the other hand, there is little more than trial by jury and basic due process.

This distinction recognizes that the stakes are generally higher in criminal cases in which a defendant can be deprived of liberty and life than in civil cases involving money. This is not always the case, since some civil judgments can bankrupt a defendant, while some criminal penalties can be trivial,

but the stigma of a criminal conviction is worse and the penalties usually more painful.

The civil-criminal distinction has gone through several
historical phases. In the beginning of recorded history, the
line was blurred, especially between torts and crimes: in both
situations the defendant has hurt the victim, and the victim
seeks recompense or revenge from the courts. In earlier days,
where there were no prisons for long-term incarceration,
the recompense was primarily economic, except in extreme
cases where only capital punishment was deemed a sufficient
remedy.

With the advent of the prison system, the separation
between civil and criminal grew sharper. More recently, the
ambit of the criminal law has expanded significantly, so that
harmful conduct once deemed only tortious began to be
treated as criminal. This is especially so with regard to negligent acts that produce great harm, such as death or serious
injury from automobile accidents, or dangerous consumer
products, such as germ-laden food or pharmaceuticals.

The same is true of gun accidents, as evidenced recently by
the involuntary manslaughter prosecution of Alec Baldwin
for accidentally killing a film set employee by shooting a prop
gun he was told had no live ammunition. An even more controversial prosecution was against Kim Potter, a police officer
who intended to stop a fleeing felon by properly shooting him
with her taser, but accidentally drew and fired her revolver,
killing him. She was convicted of first- and second-degree
manslaughter, sentenced to two years in prison, and denied
bail pending appeal, though it was undisputed that she did
not intend to shoot him with live ammunition. Some anti-
police activists wanted to charge her with murder.

Another current example of criminalizing negligent behavior is the manner by which the careless handling of classified material, such as by former president Donald Trump, current president Joe Biden, and former secretary of state Hillary Clinton. The relevant criminal statute does require evidence that the person who possesses the documents "knowingly removed" them with the intent to "retain" them, but it doesn't require proof of any intent to disclose or misuse them.

Other examples of current crimes that used to be torts involve the negligent distribution of foods and pharmaceuticals that are dangerous, and negligent failure to protect children from harm.

There are two major reasons why criminal liability has been extended to cover negligent behavior. The first is evidentiary: It is often difficult or impossible to prove a specific intent to commit a crime, so the law takes a shortcut, substituting negligence, which is far easier to prove.

The second reason is to put the burden of preventing harms on the persons most able to do so. Under this approach, Baldwin and Potter are held criminally responsible for NOT taking additional steps to assure that they were not firing lethal weapons. Those carelessly in possession of classified documents are criminally accountable for NOT being more careful. And those selling food or pharmaceuticals are required to assure the safety of their products or risk criminal prosecution.

One consequence of this expanding criminalization of what used to be civil violations is to reduce the stigma of a criminal conviction. When a specific intent to cross the line to criminality was required—a calculated decision "to be or not to be" a criminal—it was easier to differentiate the morally and legally culpable from the merely careless. Today that line has become fuzzier. Another consequence, which we are currently experiencing in the political world, is the weaponization of the criminal justice system for partisan purposes.

All in all, the unmistakable trend toward overcriminalization is a knife that cuts both ways: It may make us a bit safer, but not without real costs.

A Technological Solution to the Classification Problem

Classified documents have now been found among the papers of former president Trump, President Biden, and former vice president Pence. There is little doubt that if the offices, basements, garages, and libraries of all former presidents and vice presidents were searched, more classified material would turn up.

There's little evidence that officials who previously had access to classified material made deliberate decisions to keep them, knowing they were classified. There are exceptions of course, such as former national security adviser Sandy Berger, who willfully secreted secret material in his socks, in order to help him prepare his memoir. It is far more likely that when classified material ends up in the files of former officials, it was as a result of unawareness, sloppiness, carelessness, or inadvertence. But regardless of how or why such material ends up in unsecured areas, a national security threat may exist.

There may be a technological solution or amelioration to this ongoing problem. Scientists and technologists have devised methods of electronic tracking that may be applicable to classified material. I am neither an expert in classification nor technology, but simple common sense suggests that the stamp that is now placed on classified material can be made to contain an electronic tracking device that can identify and locate any such material. If that were done, it would be a simple matter for the archives' law enforcement officials to quickly identify classified material, bearing such a stamp, by an electronic search. Such a search could be conducted of all material leaving the White House, much like searches are today conducted at clothing and other stores in which items are electronically tagged and programmed to beep if improperly removed.

Critics may point out technical fallacies with my proposal, but if we can send men to the moon. . . .

Such a technological solution would carry several advantages: first, it would make it easier for everyone—government officials who were properly in possession of classified material, archivists who are supposed to obtain control of them, law enforcement officials investigating improper possession—to make sure that no classified material is inadvertently removed from secure places; second, it might well reduce the quantity of items that were originally classified, since more resources would have to be expended to electronically mark and designate classified items; third, classifications could be time-limited, and such limitations could be reflected in the electronic devices.

The third point, the time limitations, could be a considerable improvement to the entire process of classification. Today, an item that is marked classified remains marked classified forever. But justifications for keeping material classified change and disappear over time. Consider for example the items found among Biden's papers. Some of them go back to his Senate days, the remainder to his terms as vice president. It is very likely that much of their contents are now either public knowledge or no longer subject to classification. (That is why, Biden would be well advised to declassify whatever material he possesses that no longer requires secrecy.)

The classification system today is broken. Far too many documents are routinely classified for political and personal reasons—to avoid embarrassment, to deny access to political opponents—rather than for compelling reasons of national security. In an open and transparent democracy, there should be a strong presumption against classification and in favor of public access. Items once classified should be subject to periodic review and declassification. Very rarely should an item be classified forever, or even for long periods of time. Once declassified, the electronic device could be set not to beep.

One reason why so many public officials are so sloppy about how they handle material marked classified, is that they understand that most of these items do not really require secrecy. Many corporations and businesses do more to protect business secrets than the government does to protect what it claims are national security secrets. The recent disclosures demonstrate how sloppy, not only office holders have been, but also government officials charged with protecting our national security. We can and must do more to strike the appropriate balance between secrecy and disclosures. And we must do more to prevent the kind of inadvertent possession of classified material by former officials than we have thus far done.

So let's stop pointing partisan fingers at the past blunders of political opponents and let's take preventive measures designed to avoid future problems.

Conclusion

The illegal and unconstitutional targeting of a potential presidential candidate—the "Get Trump" campaign—will not stop with Donald Trump. Whether this anti-democratic effort to stop Trump from running succeeds or fails, it is likely to create dangerous precedents that will lie around like loaded weapons ready to be deployed against other controversial candidates, officials, or citizens about whom it can be argued that the danger they pose "is different."

Let there be little doubt that Republican zealots will seize upon any precedent established by Democratic zealots when the circumstances allow it. History proves that neither party can be trusted to apply the law neutrally and in a nonpartisan matter. Jamelle Bouie, one of the most anti-Republican partisans writing for the *New York Times*, has advocated "partisan solutions" to partisan problems. In other words, two wrongs make a right. "No! Two wrongs make a fight"—or a third wrong.

Principles cannot be counted on to prevent tit for tat retaliation in today's partisan world. Principled precedents, if observed and applied neutrally, can however function to some degree as a check on overzealous weaponization of the law. But it's a double-edged sword. Bad precedents that allow such weaponization can serve as a stimulus to such abuses.

Partisan zealots don't care about precedent because their goals are short term—immediate gratification of their political needs. The future is for others to worry about. But the future in politics is never far away. It is measured in biennial elections that can quickly hand a weaponized precedent to one's opponent. The Republicans, who now control the House, may well deploy the precedents established by the Democrats. These include broadening the reach of crimes and other sanctions such as intrusive investigations, disbarments, and civil fraud lawsuits. They also include subpoenaing and publishing the tax returns of political opponents. Republican House leaders have already stacked crucial committees with zealots who are likely to emulate the excesses of previous committees stacked in favor of Democrats. Civil libertarians who have traditionally opposed such tactics, except when directed at Trump and his associates, may well see them turned against themselves and their allies. This is the road to a banana republic, where electoral defeat results in imprisonment, bankruptcy, or worse.

I will continue to do what I have been doing for sixty years; defend the constitutional rights of all who are subject to governmental mistreatment. Over the years, I have defended the rights mostly of Democrats: Ted Kennedy,

Alan Cranston, Edwin Edwards, Bill Clinton, Al Gore, and others. These days I defend many Republicans because it is the Democrats who are in power in the Justice Department and Senate and employing unconstitutional measures against Republicans. If I live long enough, I am confident that I will once again be defending Democrats against Republicans who will be using similarly unconstitutional measures.

If and when that reversal of fortune were to occur, I would be attacked by Republicans and supported by Democrats— the mirror image of what happened when I defended Trump against an unconstitutional impeachment.

As a liberal democrat and former National Board Member of the ACLU, I am particularly concerned that the left can no longer be counted on to oppose oppression— when it comes from the left. Democrats, liberals, and civil libertarians were on the forefront of opposing the excesses of Republican administrations—most recently of George W. Bush and Donald Trump. I supported them when they did so. But now that the unconstitutional oppression is coming largely from the left, these groups are either silent or complicit. They have shown the world that their opposition to Republican oppression was partisan and tactical rather than principled and neutral. They have lost their credibility as guardians of the Constitution for all.

Today, there are precious few principled civil libertarians who will stand up equally for oppression by the left and by the right. When I have opposed unconstitutional actions against Donald Trump and his associates, many of my former liberal and civil libertarian associates have turned against me (see *The Price of Principle*). Their actions have sent a powerful message: standing for principle against one's party or ideology risks cancellation, censorship, and loss of status.

The dangers to civil liberties increase exponentially when prominent liberals and civil libertarians refuse to stand up against oppression from their friends and colleagues. That is why it is so important for liberal Democrats like me to write books like this, calling out my side for abandoning their principles in the interest of achieving short-term partisan goals. I hope this book will encourage other liberals and civil libertarians to stick by their principles. I also hope it will encourage Republicans who have been justly critical of unprincipled attacks against Democrats to stick to their principles, now that the shoe is on the other foot. History provides little basis for optimism with regard to the application of a single principled criteria. But I cannot remain silent in the face of hypocrisy, double standards, and unprincipled partisanship.

Appendix A:
The Boston Massacre Trials

I have referred repeatedly to John Adams's defense of the British soldiers accused of the Boston Massacre. I have written the following about Adams's role in that notorious case:

Date:	*1770*
Location:	*Boston, Massachusetts*
Defendants:	*Captain Thomas Preston, Corporal William Wemms, and seven British soldiers*
Charges:	*Murder, accessory to murder*
Verdict:	*Captain and corporal acquitted; two privates convicted of manslaughter*
Sentence:	*Branding*

The manner by which an event is characterized by history often determines our collective attitudes toward the culpability of the participants. The so-called Boston Massacre is a case in point. Every American schoolchild learns that British solders "massacred" several Bostonians by shooting into a crowed of patriotic protestors. It was the "real" beginning of the American Revolution, the first shots heard round the world.

A review of the actual trial records—there were two trials, the first of the commanding officer, the second of the soldiers—shows anything but an unprovoked massacre. It was much closer to an instance of arguable self-defense by a handful of frightened soldiers, cornered by a violent mob threatening to injure or kill them. Situations like this have arisen throughout—most recently in Israel and Iraq—where soldiers fire on provocateurs who engage in, or threaten, violence. The term *massacre* should be reserved for cases of unprovoked mass killing against innocent people. To be sure, the Boston case was a close one, but close cases are supposed to be resolved in favor of the defendants—at least by a court of law. The verdict of history may well be different, as it was in this case. History, especially patriotic history, thrives on mythology. And the "Boston Massacre" emerged as one of the canonical myths of prerevolutionary America.

Another myth—this one perpetrated by lawyers at bar association conventions and in Law Day speeches—is that it took enormous courage for the defense lawyers, led by future president John Adams, to defend the hated British soldiers. The evidence suggests that this was not true. The community was divided, and many upstanding citizens of Boston understood that the "rabble" that gathered in Dock Square on that cold March night with cudgels, ice balls, and other makeshift weapons comprised provocateurs who invited the violence that ensued. Maybe the soldiers overreacted; perhaps they shot too soon and did not stop quickly enough. But reasonable people could, and did, disagree as to whether this was murder, manslaughter, or self-defense. Judges and juries decided these complex factual and legal issues only after listening to the dozens of witnesses called by each side.

The trials themselves were exemplars of civility and due process, conducted professionally and brilliantly by all the lawyers. The true hero of this tragedy was the legal system—the British legal system, as administered by colonial Americans—which managed to turn a potentially explosive incident into a civics lesson about the rule of law.

Every American, especially lawyers and law students, should study this trial. The reality is far more interesting than the mythology. The closing arguments of counsel are classic instances of the advocacy of the day. Listen to John Adams:

> May it please your honors, and you, gentlemen of the jury: I am for the prisoners at the bar, and shall apologize for it only in the words of the Marquis Beccaria: "If I can but be the instrument of preserving one life, his blessing and tears of transport, shall be a sufficient consolation to me, for the contempt of all mankind." As the prisoners stand before you for their lives, it may be proper, to recollect with what temper the law requires we should proceed to this trial. The form of proceeding at their arraignment, has discovered that the spirit of the law upon such occasions, is conformable to humanity, to common sense and feeling; that it is all benignity and candor. And the trial

commences with the prayer of the court, expressed by the clerk, to the supreme judge of judges, empires and worlds: "God send you a good deliverance."

We find, in the rules laid down by the greatest English judges, who have been the brightest of mankind; we are to look upon it as more beneficial, that many guilty persons should escape unpunished, than one innocent person should suffer. The reason is, because it is for more importance to the community, that innocence should be protected, than it is, that guilt should be punished; for guilt and crimes are so frequent in the world, that all of them cannot be punished; and many times they happen in such a manner, that it is not of much consequence to the public, whether they are punished or not. But when innocence itself, is brought to the bar and condemned, especially to die, the subject will exclaim, it is immaterial to me whether I behave well or ill, for virtue itself is no security. And if such a sentiment as this should take place in the mind of the subject, there would be an end to all security whatsoever.

Not everything Adams said should be praised. He played an early version of what has come to be known as the "race card." One of those killed by the soldiers was a black man named Crispus Attucks. Adams told the all-white jury that Attucks was the one to blame for the confrontation:

Bailey "saw the mulatto seven or eight minutes before the firing, at the head of twenty or thirty sailors in Cornhill, and he had a large cord-wood stick." So that this Attucks, by the testimony of Bailey compared with that of Andrew and some others, appears to have undertaken to be the hero of the night; and to lead this army with banners, to form them in the first place in Dock square, and march them up to King street with their clubs; they passed through the main street up to the main-guard, in order to make the attack. If this was not unlawful assembly, there never was one in the world. Attucks with his myrmidons comes round Jackson's corner, and down to the party by the sentry box; when the soldiers pushed the people off, this man with his party cried, do not be afraid of them, they dare not fire, kill them! kill them! knock them over! and he tried to knock their brains out. It is plain the soldiers did not leave their station, but cried to the people, stand off; now to have this reinforcement coming down under the command of a stout mulatto fellow, whose very looks was enough to terrify any person, what had not the soldiers then to fear? He had hardiness enough to fall in upon them, and with one hand took hold of a bayonet, and with the other knocked the man down: this was the behavior of Attucks: to whose mad behavior, in all probability, the dreadful carnage of that night is chiefly to be ascribed. And it is in this manner, this town has been often treated; a Carr from Ireland, and Attucks from Framingham, happening to be here, shall sally out upon their thoughtless enterprises, at the head of such a rabble of Negroes, &c., as they can collect together, and then there are not wanting persons to ascribe all their doing to the good people of the town.

Adams also played the "God card." He consistently invoked the law of God and the Bible in support of his claim of self-defense:

> As the love of God and our neighbor, comprehends the whole duty of man, so self-love and social, comprehend all the duties we owe to mankind, and the first branch is self-love, which is not only our indisputable right, but our clearest duty; by the laws of nature, this is interwoven in the heart of every individual; God Almighty, whose laws we cannot alter, has implanted it there, and we can annihilate ourselves, as easily as root out this affection for ourselves. It is the first and strongest principle in our nature; Justice Blackstone calls it "the primary canon in the law of nature." That precept of our holy religion which commands us to love our neighbor as ourselves, doth not command us to love our neighbor better than ourselves, or so well, no Christian divine hath given this interpretation. The precept enjoins that our benevolence to our fellow men, should be as real and sincere, as our affections to ourselves, not that it should be as great in degree. A man is authorized, therefore, by common sense, and the laws of England, as well as those of nature, to love himself better than his fellow subject: if two person are cast away at sea, and get on a plank (a case put by Sir Francis Bacon), and the plank is insufficient to hold them both, the one hath a right to push the other off to save himself. The rules of the common law therefore, which authorize a man to preserve his own life at the expense of another's, are not contracted by any divine or moral law.

Finally, when two of the soldiers were convicted of man-slaughter—the officer and the other soldier were all acquit-ted—the defense team pulled the ultimate God card from the bottom of the deck. They invoked "the benefit of the clergy, which was allowed them, and thereupon they were each of them burned in the hand, in open court, and dis-charged." This "benefit" originally protected Christian cler-gymen from criminal prosecution in England's secular courts. The privilege developed over time to protect "clerks," or literate persons, from prosecution for felonies punishable by death. Here it was applied to soldiers in service of the king. It seems quite anachronistic that just a few years before the enactment of our First Amendment, a British colonial court in Boston would have allowed this archaic, religiously inspired resolution to a great political case. No wonder we fought a revolution and built a wall of separation between church and state!

Extracts: Adams' Argument for the Defense: 3–4 December 1770, National Archives, https://founders.archives.gov/documents/Adams/05-03-02-0001-0004-0016.